Coffeehouse Hits

ISBN 978-1-4584-3802-7

HAL•LEONARD®
CORPORATION

7777 W. BLUEMOUND RD. P.O. BOX 13819 MILWAUKEE, WI 53213

Visit Hal Leonard Online at
www.halleonard.com

Guitar Chord Songbook

Contents

Babylon

Words and Music by
David Gray

Melody:

Fri - day night _ an' I'm go - in' no - where,

(Capo 1st fret)

D   A   Em7   F#m11 Dmaj9/F#   G   Em

Intro |D |A |Em7 |F#m11 |
         |D |A . |Em7 |A |

Verse 1

Dmaj9/F#
Friday night an' I'm going nowhere,

G   Dmaj9/F#   G
All the lights are changing green ___ to red.

Dmaj9/F#
Turning over TV stations,

G   Dmaj9/F#   G
Situations running through my ___ head.

Dmaj9/F#   G
Looking back through time, you know, it's clear

                              Dmaj9/F#   G
That I've been blind, I've been a fool

        Dmaj9/F#   G
To open ___ up my heart to all that jealousy,

                    Dmaj9/F#   G
That bitterness, that ___ ridicule.

Chorus 1

D   A   Em   F#m11
And if you want it,   come an' get it,   for cryin' out loud.

D   A   Em   G
The love that I was   givin' you was   never in ___ doubt.

D   A   Em   A
Let go of your heart, ___ let go of your head, ___ and feel it ___ now.

D   A   Em   A
Let go of your heart, ___ let go of your head, ___ and feel it ___ now.

        Dmaj9/F# G   Dmaj9/F# G
Babylon, _____   Babylon.

Verse 2

Dmaj9/F#
Saturday I'm running wild

   G   Dmaj9/F#   G
An' all the lights are changin', red ___ to green.

Dmaj9/F#
Moving through the crowds, I'm pushin',

G   Dmaj9/F#   G
Chemicals are rushing in my bloodstream.

        Dmaj9/F#   G
Only wish ___ that you were here, you know, I'm seeing it so clear,

        Dmaj9/F# G   Dmaj9/F#
I've been a - fraid   to show ___ you how I really feel,

    G   Dmaj9/F#   G
Admit ___ to some of those bad mis - takes I've made.

              D   A   Em   F#m11
Chorus 2   Well,   if you want it,   come an' get it,   for cryin' out loud.

       D   A   Em   G
       The love that I was   givin' you was   never in ___ doubt.

       D   A   Em   A
       Let go of your heart, ___ let go of your head, ___ and feel it ___ now.

       D   A   Em   A
       Let go of your heart, ___ let go of your head, ___ and feel it ___ now.

       D   A   Em   A
       Let go of your heart, ___ let go of your head, ___ and feel ___ it.

       D   A   Em   A
       Let go of your heart, ___ let go of your head, ___ and feel it ___ now.

              Dmaj9/F# G   Dmaj9/F# G
       ‖: Babylon, _____   Babylon.   :‖

              Dmaj9/F#   G   Dmaj9/F#
       Babylon. ___ Why, ___ why, why, why, why, why?

Banana Pancakes

Words and Music by
Jack Johnson

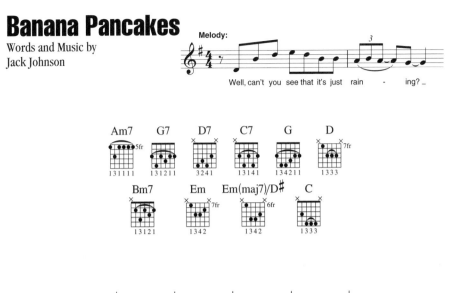

Melody:

Well, can't you see that it's just rain - ing? _

| Am7 | G7 | D7 | C7 | G | D |
| Bm7 | Em | Em(maj7)/D♯ | C |

Intro

| N.C. | Am7 | N.C. | G7 | |

N.C.   Am7
Well, can't you see that it's just raining?

N.C.   G7
There ain't no need to go out - side.

Verse 1

             D7   G7   D7
But, baby, you hardly even notice

Am7   C7   G7
When I try to show you this song,

             D7   Am7   C7
It's meant to keep you from doing what you're s'posed to.

G7   D7   Am7   C7
Waking up too early, maybe we could sleep in.

G7   D7   Am7   C7   Am7
Make you banana pancakes, pre - tend like it's the weekend now.

Chorus 1

Am7 N.C.   G7
    And we could pretend it all the time, yeah.

N.C.   Am7
Can't you see that it's just raining?

N.C.   G7
There ain't no need to go out - side.

Verse 2

        D7   G7   D7 Am7   C7
But just maybe ha - la ka uku - lele, mama made a baby.

    G7   D7   Am7   C7
I really don't mind the practice, 'cause you're my little lady.

    G7   D7   Am7   C7
Lady, lady, love me 'cause I love to lay here, lazy.

    G7   D7   Am7   C7   Am7
We could close the curtains, pre - tend like there's no world out - side.

Chorus 2

Am7 N.C.   G7
    And we could pretend it all the time, no.

N.C.   Am7
Can't you see that it's just raining?

N.C.   G7
There ain't no need to go out - side.

                Am7
Ain't no need, ain't no need.

             G7
Mm, mm, mm, mm.

                Am7
Can't you see, can't you see?

                    G
Rain all day and I don't mind.

Bridge

Am7
But the telephones singing, ringing;

D
It's too early, don't pick it up.

Am7
We don't need to; we got ev'rything we need right here

D
And ev'rything we need is enough.

Bm7
It's just so easy when the whole world fits inside of your arms.

Em   Em(maj7)/D♯ C
Do we really need to pay attention   to the alarm?

G   D7   G
Wake up slow. Mm, mm. ___ Wake up slow.

Verse 3

Repeat Verse 1

Chorus 3

Am7 N.C.   G7
   And we could pretend it all the time, yeah.

N.C.   Am7
Can't you see that it's just raining?

N.C.   G7
There ain't no need to go out - side.

Am7
Ain't no need, ain't no need.

G7
Rain all day and I real - ly, really, really don't mind.

Am7
Can't you see, can't you see?

G
We've got to wake up slow.

Beg Steal or Borrow

Words and Music by
Ray LaMontagne

Melody:

So your home - town's _ bring-in' you down. _

Tune down 1/2 step:
(low to high) Eb-Ab-Db-Gb-Bb-Eb

D   C   G   A   C/G   Fmaj7   Am7

| 132 | 32 1 | 32 4 | 123 | 342 1 | 3421 | 2 1 |

Intro   ‖: D | | C | G   :‖ *Play 3 times*
| D | G | D | G |

Verse 1

        D
So your hometown's bringin' you down.

    C   G   D   C G
Are you drownin' in the small ___ talk an' the chatter?

       D
Are you gonna step into line like your daddy done,

C   G   D   C G
Punchin' the time and climbin' life's long ___ ladder?

      D
You been howlin' at the moon like a slack-jawed fool

    C   G   D   C G
And   breakin' ev'ry rule ___ they can throw ___ on.

     D
Well, one of these days, it's gonna be right soon,

     C   G   D   C G
You'll   find your legs and go and stay ___ gone.

Chorus 1

A   C/G
Young man, full of big plans

    G   D
An' thinkin' about tomor - row.

A   C/G
Young man, gonna make a stand.

    G   Fmaj7
You beg, steal, you bor - row.

                D
You beg, you steal, ___ you borrow.

C		G		D		
	G		D		G	

Verse 2

     D
Well, all the friends that you knew in school,

    C   G
They ___ used to be so cool.

            D   C   G
Now they just bore ___ you.

     D
Well, look at 'em now, already pullin' the plow,

    C   G   D   C   G
So ___ quick to take to grain ___ like some old ___ mule.

Chorus 2

A   C/G
Young man, full of big plans

    G   D
An' thinkin' about tomor - row.

A   C/G
Young man, gonna make a stand.

    G   Fmaj7
You beg, steal, you bor - row.

You beg, you steal,

Pedal Steel Solo | D | | C | G |
You borrow.

‖: D | | C | G   :‖

| D | G | D | G |

Bridge

Am7
Dreamin' of the day you're gonna pack your bags,

           C   D
Put the miles ___ a - way.

       Am7
Oh, just grab your girl and go where no one knows you.

                 C   D   G C D
What will all the old ___ folks ___ say?

Verse 3

         D
So the hometown's bringin' you down.

     C   G   D   C G
Are you drownin' in the small ___ talk and the chatter?

            D
Are you gonna step into line like your daddy done,

    C   G   D   C G
Punchin' the time and climbin' life's long ___ ladder?

Chorus 3

A   C/G
Young man, full of big plans

 G   D
An' thinkin' about tomor - row.

A   C/G
Young man, gonna make a stand.

 G   Fmaj7
You beg, steal, you bor - row.

                 D   C G
You beg, you steal, ___ you borrow.

Outro | D | G | D |

| G | D | G | D   ‖

Black Horse and the Cherry Tree

Words and Music by
Katie Tunstall

Melody:

(Woo, hoo, ___ woo, hoo,

Em   B7   D   C

| | | |
| 2 3 | 2 1 3   4 | 1 3 2 | 3 2   1 |

Intro

| Em   B7
(Woo, hoo, woo, hoo,
Em   **B7**
  Woo, hoo, woo, hoo.)

Verse 1

     Em   N.C.
  Well, my heart knows me better than I know myself

So I'm gonna let it do all the talkin'.
    Em   B7
(Woo, hoo, woo, hoo.)
Em N.C.
  I came across a place in the middle of nowhere

With a big black horse and a cherry tree.
    Em   B7
(Woo, hoo, woo, hoo.)
Em N.C.
  I fell in fear upon my back.

I said, "Don't look back, just keep on walking."
    Em   B7
(Woo, hoo, woo, hoo.)
Em   N.C.
  When the big black horse that looked this way he said,

"Hey, lady will you marry me?"
    Em   B7
(Woo, hoo, woo, hoo.)

```
        Em              D        C
```
But I said, "No, no, ____ no, no, ____ no, no."

```
            Em      D         C                 Em
```
I said, "No, no, ____ you're ____ not the one for me.

```
            D          C
```
No, no, ____ no, no, ____ no, no."

```
            Em      D  N.C.              Em
```
I said, "No, no, ____ you're not the one for me."

(Hoo, woo, woo.)

Verse 2

```
        N.C.
```
And my heart had a problem in the early hours

So I stopped it dead for a beat or two.

```
        Em        B7
```
(Woo, hoo, woo, hoo.)

```
Em      N.C.
```
But I cut some cord and I shouldn't have done that,

And it won't forgive me after all these years.

```
        Em        B7
```
(Woo, hoo, woo, hoo.)

```
Em      N.C.
```
So I sent her to a place in the middle of nowhere

With a big black horse and a cherry tree.

```
        Em        B7
```
(Woo, hoo, woo, hoo.)

```
Em        N.C.
```
Now it won't come back 'cause it's oh, so happy

And now I got a hole for the world to see.

```
        Em        B7
```
(Woo, hoo, woo, hoo.)

Chorus 2

```
Em                  D           C
And it said, "No, no, ____ no, no, ____ no, no."
        Em      D          C                    Em
It said, "No, no, ____ you're ____ not the one for me.
        D           C
No, no, ____ no, no, ____ no, no."
        Em      D  N.C.              N.C.(Em)
It said, "No, no, ____ you're not the one for me."
                                    (Hoo, woo, hoo.)
```

Not the one for me, yeah.
                (Hoo, woo, hoo.)

```
        N.C.
It said, "No, no, no, no, no, no, no,
```

No, no, you're not the one for me.

(Woo, hoo,   woo, hoo,)
   No, no, no, no,   no, no, no,

(Woo, hoo.) No, no, you're not the one for me.

Outro

```
Em       D              C
  Big black horse and a cherry tree.
Em                 D
  I can't quite get ____ there
          C                Em
'Cause my heart's forsaken me, ____ yeah, yeah, yeah.
        D    C                 Em
Big black horse   and a cherry tree.
                    D              C  N.C.
I can't quite get ____ there 'cause my heart's forsaken me.
```

Burn One Down

Words and Music by
Ben Harper

Melody:

Let us __ burn one   from end to end,

Tune down 1 step:
(low to high) D-G-C-F-A-D

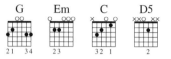

G   Em   C   D5

Intro
‖: G | :‖ *Play 5 times*

Verse 1

G
Let us burn one from end to end,

Em   C
And pass it over to me, my friend.

G
Burn it long, we'll burn it slow

Em   C
To light me up be - fore I go.

Chorus 1

          G   Em
If you don't like my fire, then don't come around

              D5   C G
'Cause I'm gonna burn one down.

          Em   D5   C   G
Yes, I'm ___ gonna burn ___ one   dow-ha-ha-how-down.

Interlude
‖: G | | | :‖

Verse 2

      G
My choice is what I choose to do.

      Em   **C**
And if I'm causin' no harm, it shouldn't bother you.

      G
Your choice is who you choose to be.

      Em   **C**
And if you're causin' no harm, then you're alright with me.

Chorus 2   *Repeat Chorus 1*

Interlude 2   *Repeat Interlude 1*

Verse 3

      G
Herb, the gift from the earth,

      Em   **C**
And what's from the earth is of the greatest worth.

      G
So be - fore you knock it, try it first.

      Em   **C**
Oh, you'll see it's a blessing and it's not a curse.

Chorus 3

      G   **Em**
If you don't like my fire, then don't come around

      D5   **C** **G**
'Cause I'm gonna burn one down.

      Em   **D5**   **C**
Yes, I'm ___ gonna burn ___ one. ___ *Aw.*

Outro   ‖: G | | | :‖ ***Repeat and fade***

Chasing Cars

Words and Music by Gary Lightbody,
Tom Simpson, Paul Wilson,
Jonathan Quinn and Nathan Connolly

Melody:

We'll do — it ___ all, _____

A5   E/G#   Dsus2   A5*   E/G#*   D5/A

Intro

| A5 | | |

Verse 1

        A5   E/G#   Dsus2   A5
We'll do it all,   ev'rything ___ on our own.

              E/G#   Dsus2   A5
We don't need   anything ___ or anyone.

Chorus 1

        A5   E/G#
If I lay here, if I just lay here,

             Dsus2   A5
Would you lie with me and just forget the world?

Verse 2

      A5   E/G#   Dsus2   A5
I don't quite know   how to say ___ how I feel.

              E/G#   Dsus2   A5
Those three words,   I said too much, ___ then not enough.

Chorus 2

A5   E/G#
If I lay here, if I just lay here,

Dsus2   A5
Would you lie with me and just forget the world?

Verse 3

A5   E/G#
Forget what we're told before we get too ___ old.

Dsus2   A5
Show me a garden that's bursting into life.

E/G#   Dsus2   A5
Let's waste time ___ chasing cars ___ around our heads.

E/G#   Dsus2   A5
I need your grace ___ to remind me ___ to find my own.

Chorus 3

A5*   E/G#*
If I lay here, if I just lay here,

D5/A   A5*
Would you lie with me and just forget the world?

Verse 4

A5*   E/G#*
Forget what we're told before we get too ___ old.

D5/A   A5*
Show me a garden that's bursting into life.

E/G#*
All that I am, all that I ever was

D5/A   A5*
Is here in your perfect eyes, they're all I can see.

E/G#*
I don't know where, confused about how as well.

D5/A   A5*
Just know that these things will never change for us at all.

Outro-Chorus   *Repeat Chorus 1*

Come On Get Higher

Words and Music by
Matt Nathanson and Mark Weinberg

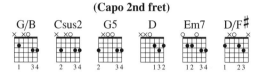

I miss the sound of your _ voice, _

(Capo 2nd fret)

G/B   Csus2   G5   D   Em7   D/F#

Intro
‖: G/B Csus2 | G5   :‖

Verse 1

G/B   Csus2   G5
I miss the sound of your voice,

G/B   Csus2   G5
And I miss the rush of your skin.

G/B   Csus2 G5
And I miss the still of the si - lence

        G/B   Csus2   D
As you ___ breathe out,   and I ___ breathe in.

Pre-Chorus 1

          Csus2   G5
If I could walk on water, if I could tell you what's next,

    Em7   D
I'd make you believe, I'd make you forget.

Chorus 1

Csus2   G5
So, come on, get higher. Loosen my lips.

Csus2   G5
Faith ___ and desire in the swing of your hips.

Csus2   G5   Em7   D/F♯
Just pull me down hard   and drown ___ me in love.

Csus2   G5
So, come on, get higher. Loosen my lips.

Csus2   G5
Faith ___ and desire in the swing of your hips.

Csus2   G5   Em7   D/F♯
Just pull me down hard   and drown ___ me in love.

Verse 2

G/B   Csus2   G5
I miss the sound of your voice,

G/B   Csus2   G5
The loudest thing in my head.

G/B   Csus2   G5
And I ache ___ to remem - ber

G/B   Csus2   D
All the vi - olent, sweet, perfect words ___ that you said.

Pre-Chorus 2   *Repeat Pre-Chorus 1*

Chorus 2   *Repeat Chorus 1*

Bridge

Csus2
I miss the pull of your heart.

Em7
I taste the sparks on your tongue.

G5   D   Csus2
And I see angels and dev - ils and God when you come ___ on.

Em7   D
Hold ___ on, hold on, ___ hold on, hold on, love.

Interlude

G/B Csus2   G5
       Sing, sha, la, la, la.

G/B Csus2   G5
       Sing, sha, la, la, la, la.

   G/B Csus2   G5
Hoo, _____ hoo.

    G/B   Csus2   D
Hoo, ___ oo, hoo, ___ hoo,   oo.

Chorus 3

Csus2   G5
Come on, get higher. Loosen my lips.

   Csus2   G5
Faith ___ and desire in the swing of your hips.

   Csus2   G5   Em7   D/F♯
Just pull me down hard   and drown ___ me in love.

   Csus2   G5
So, come on, get higher. Loosen my lips.

   Csus2   G5
Faith ____ and desire in the swing of your hips.

Csus2   G5   Em7   D/F♯
Pull me down hard   and drown ___ me, drown me in love.

Outro

   Csus2   G5   Csus2 G5
(Come on, get higher…) It's all wrong. _____ It's all wrong.

   Csus2   G5 Em7
(Pull me down hard…) It's all _____ right.

D/F♯   Csus2   G5   Csus2   G5
So, come on, ___ get high - er. Come on, ___ get high - er.

     Csus2   G5   Em7
'Cause ev' - rything works, love, ev' - rything works

D/F♯ Csus2
In your ___ arms.

Elderly Woman Behind the Counter in a Small Town

Words and Music by Stone Gossard,
Jeffrey Ament, Eddie Vedder, Michael McCready
and David Abbruzzese

Melody:

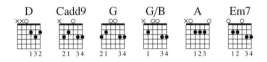

Verse 1

   D Cadd9 G   Cadd9 G/B
I   seem to recognize your face.

D   Cadd9 G/B
Haunt - ing, famil - iar,

           Cadd9 G/B
Yet I can't seem to place it.

D   Cadd9   G/B
Cannot find ____ a can - dle of thought

       Cadd9   G/B G
To light ____ your name.

D   Cadd9   G/B   Cadd9 G/B
Life - times are catching up with me.

Pre-Chorus 1

Cadd9 A   Cadd9
All these changes taking place,

   A   Cadd9
I wish I'd seen the place,

    A   Em7
But no one's ever taken me.

Chorus 1	D **Cadd9** **G**

Chorus 1

D **Cadd9** **G**
Hearts and thoughts, they fade,

Cadd9 G
Fade a - way.

D **Cadd9** **G**
Hearts and thoughts, they fade,

Cadd9 G
Fade a - way.

Verse 2

D Cadd9 G/B   **Cadd9 G/B**
I swear I recognize your breath.

D   **Cadd9** **G/B**
Memories, ___ like fingerprints,

 Cadd9 G/B G
Are slowly rais - ing.

D **Cadd9** **G/B**
Me, you wouldn't recall,

  Cadd9 G/B **G**
For I'm not my form - er.

D   **Cadd9** **G/B**   **Cadd9 G/B**
It's hard when you're stuck upon the shelf.

Pre-Chorus 2

Cadd9   **A**   **Cadd9**
I changed by not changing at all,

  A   **Cadd9**
Small town predicts my fate,

  A   **Em7**
Per - haps that's what no one wants to see.

Bridge

      D   Cadd9 G/B   Cadd9 G/B
Uh, I just want to scream, "Hello!"

D Cadd9 G/B
My God, it's been so long,

      Cadd9   G/B G
Never dreamed you'd re - turn,

D   Cadd9 G/B
But now here you are,

      Cadd9 G/B
And here I   am.

D   Cadd9   G/B   Cadd9 G/B
Hearts and thoughts, ___ they fade ___ away.

Chorus 2

D   Cadd9   G
Hearts and thoughts, they fade,

Cadd9 G
Fade a - way.

D   Cadd9   G
Hearts and thoughts, they fade,

Cadd9 G
Fade a - way.

D   Cadd9   G Cadd9 G
Hearts and thoughts, they fade a   -   way.

D   Cadd9   G
Hearts and thoughts, they fade,

Cadd9 G
Fade a - way.

Outro

D   Cadd9   G/B
Hearts and thoughts, they fade,

Cadd9 G/B
Fade a - way.

D   Cadd9   G/B
Hearts and thoughts, they fade,

Cadd9 G/B G
Fade a - way.

D   Cadd9   G
Hearts and thoughts, they fade.   *Fade out*

Come Pick Me Up

Words and Music by
Ryan Adams and Van Alston

Melody:

When they call ___ your name, ___

(Capo 3rd fret)

G   Em7   C   Am   Gadd4/B   D   G/B

Intro

‖: G   Em7 | C | G   Em7 | C   :‖

Verse 1

    G   Em7
When they call your name,

                      C   Am
Will you walk right up   with a smile on your face?

    G   Em7
Will you cower in fear

                         C   Am
In your fav'rite sweater, ___ with an old love letter?

Pre-Chorus 1

Am   Gadd4/B   C
I wish ___ you would,

Am   Gadd4/B   C
I wish ___ you would…

Chorus 1

                     G   C
Come pick me up, ___ take me out,

            Am   C
Fuck me up, ___ steal my records,

                    G   C
Screw all my friends; ___ they're all full of shit.

                        Am   C
With a smile on your face, ___ and then do it again.

D   G Em7 C G Em7 C
I wish you would.

Verse 2

```
G                              Em7
  When you're walkin' downtown,
                         C                      Am
Do you wish I was there? ___ Do you wish it was me?
G                    Em7
  With the windows clear,
                         C                      Am
In the mannequin's eyes, ___ do they all look like mine?
```

Pre-Chorus 2

```
Am        Gadd4/B      C
  You know ___ you could,
Am     Gadd4/B      C
  I wish ___ you would...
```

Chorus 2

```
                        G              C
Come pick me up, ___ take me out,
                  Am            C
Fuck me up, ___ steal my records,
                        G             C
Screw all my friends ___ behind my back.
                         Am                 C
With a smile on your face, ___ and then do it again.
D
  I wish you would.
```

Harmonica Solo

```
‖: G   Em7  | C        | G   Em7  | C        :‖
```

Bridge

```
D                  G/B     C
  I wish you'd make up my bed
D             G/B      C
  So I could make up my mind,
D               G/B     C
  Try it for sleep - in' instead.
D               G/B       C
  Maybe you'll rest    sometime.
```

Outro

```
            G Em7  C
I wish I could.
            G Em7  C
I wish I could.
            G Em7  C
I wish I could.
| G    Em7  | C        | G            ‖
```

Constant Craving

Words and Music by K.D. Lang
and Ben Mink

Melody:

E - ven through the ___ dark - est

(Capo 3rd fret)

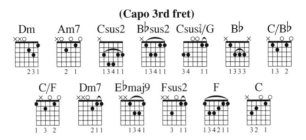

Dm Am7 Csus2 B♭sus2 Csus⁴/G B♭ C/B♭

C/F Dm7 E♭maj9 Fsus2 F C

Intro
‖: Dm | Am7 | Csus2 | B♭sus2 |
| Dm | Am7 | Csus⁴/G | | :‖

Verse 1

Dm Am7   Csus2   B♭sus2
E - ven through the ___ darkest phase,

Dm Am7   Csus⁴/G
Be   it   thick or ___ thin,

Dm Am7   Csus2   B♭sus2
Al - ways someone ___ marches brave

Dm   Am7   Csus⁴/G
Here be - neath my ___ skin.

Pre-Chorus 1

B♭ C/B♭ C/F Dm7 E♭maj9 Dm
Con-stant   crav - ing has always _____ been.

Verse 2

Dm Am7   Csus2   B♭sus2
May - be a great ___ magnet pulls

Dm Am7   Csus¾/G
All   souls towards ___ truth.

Dm   Am7   Csus2   B♭sus2
  Or may-be it is ___ life it-self

　　　　Dm   Am7   Csus¾/G
That feeds wisdom ___ to its ___ youth.

Pre-Chorus 2   *Repeat Pre-Chorus 1*

Chorus 1   **Fsus2 B♭sus2   Fsus2   F   B♭sus2**
Crav   -   ing. Ah, ah, _____ constant craving

　　　C   B♭   C   B♭
Has always ___ been, has al - ways been.

Instrumental   *Repeat Intro*

Pre-Chorus 3   *Repeat Pre-Chorus 1*

Pre-Chorus 4   **B♭ C/B♭ C/F   Dm7   E♭maj9   F**
Con-stant   crav - ing has always   been.

Chorus 2   **Fsus2 B♭sus2   Fsus2   F   B♭sus2**
Crav   -   ing. Ah, ah, _____ constant craving

　　　　C   B♭   C   B♭
‖: Has always ___ been, has always ___ been. :‖ *Repeat and fade*

Don't Know Why

Words and Music by
Jesse Harris

Melody:

I wait-ed till ___ I saw _____ the sun. ___

(Capo 6th fret)

Emaj7 E7 E Amaj7 E+ C#m7 F#7 B7sus4 B9sus4

E* C#m7* F#13 B7 B7* B7/A B7/G# B7/F#

Intro

| Emaj7 E7 E | Amaj7 E+ | C#m7 F#7 B7sus4 | B9sus4 |

Verse 1

Emaj7 E7 E   Amaj7   E+
I waited till I ____ saw ____ the sun.

C#m7   F#7   B7sus4   E*
 I don't know why ____ I did - n't come.

Emaj7 E7 E   Amaj7 E+
 I left you by ____ the house ____ of fun.

C#m7   F#7   B7sus4   E*
 I don't know why ____ I did - n't come,

C#m7   F#7   B7sus4   E*
I don't know why ____ I did - n't come.

Verse 2

Emaj7 E7 E   Amaj7 E+
 When I saw ____ the break ____ of day,

C#m7   F#7   B7sus4   E*
 I wished that I ____ could fly ____ away

Emaj7 E7 E Amaj7   E+
 'Stead of kneel - ing in ____ the sand

C#m7   F#7   B7sus4 E*
Catching tear - drops in my hand.

Bridge 1

C#m7*   F#13   B7
My heart is drenched ___ in wine,

   C#m7*   F#13   B7* B7/A B7/G# B7/F#
But you'll be on ___ my mind ___ for - ev - er.

Verse 3

Emaj7 E7   E   Amaj7   E+
  Out across ___ the end - less sea,

C#m7   F#7 B7sus4 E*
  I would die ___ in ecstasy.

Emaj7 E7 E   Amaj7   E+
  But I'll be ___ a bag ___ of bones

C#m7   F#7   B7sus4 E*
Driving down ___ the road ___ alone.

Bridge 2

C#m7*   F#13   B7
  My heart is drenched ___ in wine,

  C#m7* F#13   B7
But you'll be on ___ my mind ___ forever.

Piano Solo

‖: Emaj7 E7 E │ Amaj7 E+ │ C#m7 F#7 B9sus4 │   :‖

Verse 4

Emaj7   E7   E   Amaj7   E+
  Something has ___ to make ___ you run.

C#m7   F#7   B7sus4   E*
  I don't know why ___ I did - n't come.

  Emaj7 E7   E Amaj7   E+
I   feel as empty ___ as ___ a drum.

C#m7   F#7 B7sus4   E*
  I don't know why ___ I did - n't come,

  C#m7   F#7   B7sus4   E*
I   don't know why ___ I did - n't come.

  C#m7   F#7   B7sus4   E*
I ___ don't know why ___ I did - n't come.

Fallin' for You

Words and Music by
Colbie Caillat and Rick Nowels

Melody:

I don't know, _ but   I think I ___ may

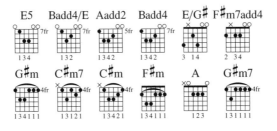

| E5 | Badd4/E | Aadd2 | Badd4 | E/G# | F#m7add4 |

| G#m | C#m7 | C#m | F#m | A | G#m7 |

Intro ‖: E5 | Badd4/E | Aadd2 | Badd4 :‖

Verse 1

    E5   Badd4/E
    I don't know,   but I think

            Aadd2   Badd4
I may be ___ fallin' for you,   droppin' so quickly.

    E5   Badd4/E   Aadd2
    Maybe I should   keep this to myself,

            Badd4
Wait until I   know you better.

Pre-Chorus 1

          Aadd2   E/G#   F#m7add4
I am tryin' not to tell you, but I want to.

          E/G#
I'm scared ___ of what you'll say,

         Aadd2   G#m C#m7
And so I'm hidin' what I'm feelin',

        F#m7add4 E/G# Aadd2   Badd4
But I'm tired ___ of   hold - ing this in - side my head.

Chorus 1

    E5   Badd4/E
I've been spendin' all my   time just thinkin' 'bout you.

Aadd2   Badd4
I don't know what to do.   I think I'm fallin' for you.

E5   Badd4/E
I've been waitin' all my   life, and now I've found you.

Aadd2   Badd4   E5
I don't know what to do.   I think I'm fallin' for you.

Badd4/E   Aadd2 Badd4
I'm fallin' for you.

Verse 2

E5   Badd4/E   Aadd2
As we're standin' here ____ and you hold my hand,

                    Badd4
Pull me towards you   and we start to dance.

E5   Badd4/E
All around us,   I see nobody.

Aadd2   Badd4
Here in silence,   it's just you and me.

Pre-Chorus 2   *Repeat Pre-Chorus 1*

Chorus 2   *Repeat Chorus 1*

Bridge

C#m
Oh, I just can't take it.

F#m
My heart is racin'.

A   G#m7   Badd4
Emotions keep spillin' out.

Chorus 3

E5   Badd4/E
I've been spendin' all my time just thinkin' 'bout you.

Aadd2   Badd4
I don't know what to do. I think I'm fallin' for you.

E5   Badd4/E
I've been waitin' all my life, and now I've found you.

Aadd2   Badd4   E5
I don't know what to do. I think I'm fallin' for you.

Badd4/E   Aadd2 Badd4
I'm fallin' for you. _____ I think I'm fallin' for you.

Outro

 E5
‖: I can't stop thinkin' 'bout it.

Badd4/E
I want you all around me.

Aadd2
And now I just can't hide it.

Badd4   E5
I think I'm fallin' for you. :‖

Badd4/E   Aadd2 Badd4 E5
I'm fallin' for you. _____ Oh, oh.

   Badd4/E   Aadd2
Oh, no, ___ no. Oh, oh, oh, ___ oh, oh.

Badd4   E5
Oh, I'm fallin' for ___ you.

Fast Car

Words and Music by
Tracy Chapman

Melody:

You got a fast ___ car,

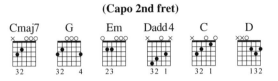

(Capo 2nd fret)

Cmaj7   G   Em   Dadd4   C   D

Intro   ‖: **Cmaj7   G |Em   Dadd4** :‖ *Play 4 times*

Verse 1

Cmaj7   G
You got a fast ___ car,

Em   Dadd4
I want a ticket ____ to anywhere.

Cmaj7   G
Maybe we make a deal,

Em   Dadd4
Maybe together we can get somewhere.

Cmaj7   G
Anyplace is better.

Em   Dadd4
Starting from zero, got nothing to lose.

Cmaj7   G
Maybe we'll make something;

Em   Dadd4
Me, myself, I got nothing to prove.

| *Interlude 1* | ‖: Cmaj7　　G　　|Em　　Dadd4　:‖ |

| *Verse 2* | **Cmaj7　　G**
You got a fast __ car,
Em　　　　Dadd4
I got a plan ____ to get us out of here.
　　Cmaj7　　　　　G
I been working at the con-venience store,
Em　　　　Dadd4
Managed to save just a little bit of money.
Cmaj7　　　　G
Won't have to drive too far,
　　Em　　　　　Dadd4
Just 'cross the border and into the city.
Cmaj7　　G
You and I can both get jobs
　　Em　　　Dadd4
And finally see what it means to be living. |

| *Interlude 2* | *Repeat Interlude 1* |

| *Verse 3* | 　　**Cmaj7　　　　G**
You see, my old man's got a problem.
　Em　　　　Dadd4
He live with the bottle, that's the way it is.
　　Cmaj7　　　G
He says his body's too old for working;
　Em　　　Dadd4
His body's too young ____ to look like his.
Cmaj7　　G
My mama went off and left him;
　Em　　　　Dadd4
She wanted more from life than he could give.
　Cmaj7　　　　G
I said somebody's got to take care of him.
　Em　　　Dadd4
So I quit school and that's what I did. |

Interlude 3	*Repeat Interlude 1*

Verse 4

Cmaj7   G
You got a fast __ car,

      Em   Dadd4
But is it fast enough so we can fly away?

Cmaj7   G
We gotta make a decision:

Em   Dadd4
Leave tonight or live and die this way.

|Cmaj7   G |Em   Dadd4 |Cmaj7   G |

Em   Dadd4
   'Cause I remember when we were...

Chorus 1

C
Driving, driving in your car,

   G
The speed so fast I felt like I was drunk.

Em
   City lights lay out before us

      D
And your arm felt nice wrapped 'round my shoulder.

   C Em   D
And I,   I had a feeling that I belonged.

C Em   D
I,   I had a feeling I could be someone,

C   D
Be someone,   be someone.

Interlude 4	*Repeat Interlude 1*

	Cmaj7 G
Verse 5	You got a fast __ car.

Em   Dadd4
We go cruising to entertain ourselves.

   Cmaj7   G
You still ain't got a job

     Em   Dadd4
And I work in a market as a checkout girl.

Cmaj7   G
I know things will get better;

Em   Dadd4
You'll find work and I'll get promoted.

Cmaj7   G
We'll move out of the shelter,

Em   Dadd4
Buy a big house and live in the suburbs.

|Cmaj7   G |Em   Dadd4 |Cmaj7   G |

Em   Dadd4
  'Cause I remember when we were...

Chorus 2	*Repeat Chorus 1*
Interlude 5	*Repeat Interlude 1*

Verse 6

Cmaj7   G

You got a fast __ car.

Em   Dadd4

I got a job that pays all our bills.

     Cmaj7   G

You stay out drinking   late at the bar;

     Em   Dadd4

See more of your friends than you do of your kids.

Cmaj7   G

I'd always hoped for better;

      Em   Dadd4

Thought maybe together   you and me'd find it.

 Cmaj7   G

I got no plans, I ain't going nowhere,

     Em   Dadd4

So take your fast car and keep on driving.

│Cmaj7 G │Em Dadd4 │Cmaj7 G   │

Em   Dadd4

  'Cause I remember when we were...

Chorus 3   *Repeat Chorus 1*

Interlude 6   *Repeat Interlude 1*

Verse 7

Cmaj7   G

You got a fast __ car.

     Em   Dadd4

Is it fast enough so you can fly away?

Cmaj7   G

You gotta make a decision:

Em   Dadd4

Leave tonight or live and die this way.

Outro   ‖: Cmaj7 G │Em   Dadd4 :‖ *Play 3 times*

              │ Cmaj7 G   ‖

Flake

Words and Music by
Jack Johnson

Melody:

I know she said it's al - right,

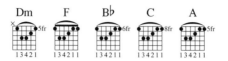

Dm   F   Bb   C   A

Intro |Dm |F |Bb |F |

Verse 1

Dm   F
I know she said it's al - right,
Bb   F
   But you can make it up next time.
Dm   F
I know she knows it's not ___ right,
Bb   F
   There ain't no use in ly-ing.
Dm   F
Maybe she thinks I know ___ something,
        Bb   F
Maybe, may-be she thinks it's fine.
Dm   F
Maybe she knows something ___ I don't.
      Bb   C
I'm so,   I'm so tired,   I'm so tired of trying.

Chorus 1

F   C
   It seems to me that "may - be,"
Dm   A
   It pretty much always means ___ "no."
      Bb   C   F   C
So don't ___ tell me you might just let it go.
F   C
   And often times we're la - zy,
Dm   A
   It seems to stand in my ___ way.
      Bb   C   F   C
'Cause no one, no, not no ___ one likes to be let down.

GUITAR CHORD SONGBOOK

	Dm F
Verse 2	I know she loves the sun - rise,

Dm   F
I know she loves the sun - rise,

B♭   F
  No longer sees it with her sleeping eyes, and

Dm   F
  I know that when she said she's gonna try,

           B♭   F
Well, it might   not work because of other ties, and,

Dm   F
  I know she usually has some other ties and, ah,

B♭
  I wouldn't want to break 'em, nah,

F
  I wouldn't want to break 'em.

Dm   F
  Maybe she'll help me to untie this, but

B♭   C
  Until then, well,   I'm gonna have to lie, too.

Chorus 2

F   C
  It seems to me that "may - be,"

Dm   A
  It pretty much always means ___ "no."

      B♭   C   F   C
So don't ___ tell me you might just let it go.

F   C
  And often times we're la - zy,

Dm   A
  It seems to stand in my ___ way.

      B♭   C   F   C
'Cause no one, no, not no ___ one likes to be let down.

F   C
  It seems to me that "may - be,"

Dm   A
  It pretty much always means ___ "no."

      B♭   C   F   C
So don't ___ tell me you might just let it go.

Dobro Solo ‖: **F** | | | :‖

Outro

F   **B♭**
The harder that you try, baby, the further you'll fall,

          F   **C**
Even with all ___ the money in the whole ___ wide world.

F
Please, please, please don't pass me,

B♭
Please, please, please don't pass me,

C   **B♭**   **F**
Please, please, please don't pass me by.

Ev'rything you know about me now, baby,

               B♭
 You gonna have to change,

              F   **C**
You gonna call ___ it by a brand new name, ___ oo, oo, oo.

F
Please, please, please don't drag me,

B♭
Please, please, please don't drag me,

C   **B♭**   **F**
Please, please, please don't drag me down.

                                   B♭
Just like a tree down by the water, baby, I shall not move,

             F   **C**
Even after all ___ the silly things you do, ___ oo, oo, oo.
F
Please, please, please don't drag me,
B♭

Please, please, please don't drag me,
C   **B♭**   **F**
Please, please, please don't drag me down.

Fugitive

Words and Music by
Robbie Malone, Keith Prior
and David Gray

Melody:

Is the an-swer "none of the a-bove,"

(Capo 5th fret)

C   G   D   Am   Em   G7/F

Intro

‖: C | |G |D :‖

Verse 1

    C
Is the answer "none of the above,"

                             G   D
Crouched in a hole like a mud streaked fugitive,

    C
Ev'ry day a diff'rent version

                              G   D
Of pouring it away like water through a sieve?

Chorus 1

    C
Hey, ___ better realize, my friend,

    Am   Em
Lord, ___ in the end now you can't take it with,

    D
Gotta live.

G   G7/F   Em
  If only for a second,   I see it twinkling in your eye.

    D
Gotta try.

Verse 2

        C
Well, it's flesh and blood and camouflage

                                    G D
Into the wall now something's gotta give.

        C
Just an - other act of sabotage

                                    G D
Seen through the haze of a mind rot sedative.

Chorus 2

        C
When ___ will you realize, my friend,

    Am   **Em**
Lord, ___ in the end now you can't take it with,

      D
Gotta live.

G   **G7/F**   **Em**
If only for a second,   I see it twinkling in your eye.

      D
Gotta try.

G
The world that you're forsaking

G7/F   **Em**
Is surely more than just a lie.

      D
Gotta try. ___ Yeah.

Slide Guitar Solo   *Repeat Verse 1 (Instrumental)*

Chorus 3

        C
Hey, ____ better realize, my friend,

  Am   **Em**
Lord, ____ in the end now you can't take it with,

     D
Gotta live.

G   **G7/F**   **Em**
If only for a second,   I see it twinkling in your eye.

     D
Gotta try.

G   **G7/F**   **Em**
The world that you're forsaking   is surely more than just a lie.

     D
Gotta try.

G   **G7/F**   **Em**
It's all there for the taking,   and you don't have to justify.

     D
Gotta try.

        C   **Am**   **Em**
Ev'ry day ____ is a diff - 'rent version of.

Half of My Heart

Words and Music by
John Mayer

Melody:

I was born ____ in the arms ____

Bb   F   C   Dm7   Dm7*   Am7   Cm7   Gm7

1 3 3 3   T 3 2 1 1   1 3 3 3   3 1 4 1   1 3 1 2 1   2 1   1 3 1 2 1   T 3 1 1 1

Intro
| Bb F C | Dm7 | Bb F C | |
| Bb F C | Dm7 | Bb | |

Verse 1

Bb   F   C
I was ____ born in the arms

    Dm7   Bb   F C
Of i - maginary ____ friends;

Bb   F   C
Free to ____ roam, made a home

    Dm7   Bb   F C
Out of ev'rywhere I've ____ been.

Pre-Chorus 1

    Bb   F   C   Dm7
Then ____ you come crashing in ____ like the real - est thing.

    Bb   F   C
Try'n' ____ my best to understand ____ all that your love ____ can bring.

Chorus 1

B♭   F
Oh, half of my heart's

     C   Dm7
Got a grip on the situation,

B♭   F   C
Half of my heart takes time.

B♭   F
Half of my heart's

     C   Dm7
Got a right mind to tell you

     B♭
That I can't keep loving you, (Can't keep loving you.)

     C
Oh, with half of my heart.

|F   C |Dm7* B♭ |F   C |Dm7* B♭ |

Verse 2

B♭   F   C
   I was ___ made to be - lieve

     Dm7   B♭   F   C
I'd never love somebody ___ else.

B♭   F   C
   Made a ___ plan, stay the man

     Dm7   B♭   F   C
Who can only love him - self.

Pre-Chorus 2

     B♭   F
Lone - ly was the song I sang

     C   Dm7
Till the day ___ you came,

     B♭   F
Show - ing me another way,

     C
And all that my love ___ can bring.

B♭   **F**
Oh, half of my heart's

   C   **Dm7**
Got a grip on the situation,

B♭   **F**   **C**
Half of my heart takes time.

B♭   **F**
Half of my heart's

   C   **Dm7**
Got a right mind to tell you

    B♭
That I can't keep loving you, (Can't keep loving you.)

              C   **F** **C**
Oh, with half of my heart.

Dm7   **B♭**   **F** **C** **Dm7** **B♭**
  With half of my heart.

Bridge

      F   **Am7**
Your faith ＿＿ is strong

    Cm7   **Gm7**
But I can only fall short for so long.

         F   **Am7**   **Cm7**
Down the road, ＿＿ later on, ＿＿ you will hate that I never

  Gm7   **B♭**
Gave more to you than half of my heart,

   C
But I can't stop loving you, (I can't stop loving you.)

  B♭
I can't stop loving you, (I can't stop loving you.)

  C
I can't stop loving you with half of my,

B♭   **F**   **C** **Dm7**
Half of my heart,

  B♭   **F** **C**
Oh, half of my heart.

Outro-Chorus

B♭   **F**
Half of my heart's

     C   **Dm7**
Got a real good imagination,

B♭   **F**   **C**
Half of my heart's got you.

B♭   **F**   **C**
Half of my heart's got a right mind

Dm7   **B♭**   **F**   **C**
To tell you that half of my heart won't do.

B♭   **F**   **C**   **Dm7**
Half of my heart is a shotgun wedding

     B♭   **F**   **C**
To a bride ___ with a paper ring.

     B♭   **F**   **C**   **Dm7**
And half of my heart is the part of a man

     B♭   **F**   **C**
Who's never truly loved anything.

B♭   **F**   **C**
Half of my heart,

Dm7 B♭   **F**   **C**
Oh, half of my heart.

B♭   **F**   **C**
Half of my heart,

Dm7 B♭   **F**   **C**
Oh, half of my heart.   *Fade out*

Hallelujah

Words and Music by
Leonard Cohen

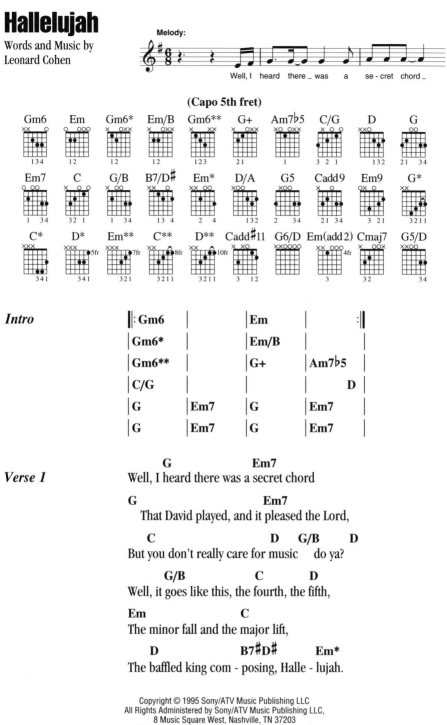

(Capo 5th fret)

Intro

‖: Gm6 | | Em | | :‖
Gm6*		Em/B		
Gm6**		G+	Am7♭5	
C/G				D
G	Em7	G	Em7	
G	Em7	G	Em7	

Verse 1

        G   Em7
Well, I heard there was a secret chord

   G   Em7
That David played, and it pleased the Lord,

      C   D G/B   D
But you don't really care for music   do ya?

       G/B   C   D
Well, it goes like this, the fourth, the fifth,

Em   C
The minor fall and the major lift,

     D   B7♯D♯   Em*
The baffled king com - posing, Halle - lujah.

Chorus 1	**D/A C** **Em** Hal - le - lujah, Halle - lujah.
	C **G D/A G5 Em7 G Em7** Halle - lujah, Halle - lu - jah.
Verse 2	**G** **Em7** Well, your faith was strong but you needed proof.
	G **Em7** You saw her bathing on the roof.
	C **D G/B D** Her beauty and the moonlight over - threw ya.
	G/B **C** **D** As she tied you to her kitchen chair,
	Em **C** As she broke your throne and she cut your hair,
	D **B7/D♯** **Em*** And from your lips you drew the Halle - lujah.
Chorus 2	*Repeat Chorus 1*
Verse 3	**G** **Em7** My baby, I've been here before.
	G **Em7** I've seen this room and I've walked this floor.
	C **D G/B D** You know, I used to live alone be - fore I knew ya.
	G/B **C** **D** And I've seen your flag on the marble arch,
	Em **C** And love is not a vict'ry march,
	D **B7/D♯** **Em*** It's a cold and it's a broken Halle - lujah.
Chorus 3	*Repeat Chorus 1*

Verse 4

       G   **Em7**
Well, there was a time when you let me know

G   **Em7**
  What's really going on below,

     C   **D**   **G/B**   **D**
But now you never show that to me, do ya?

    G/B   **C**   **D**
But, remember when I moved in you,

Em   **C**
And the Holy Dove was moving too,

     D   **B7/D**♯   **Em***
And ev'ry breath we drew was Halle - lujah.

Chorus 4

    D/A **C**   **Em**
Hal - le - lujah, Halle - lujah.

       C   **G** **D/A**
Halle - lujah, Halle - lu - jah.

Interlude

Cadd9	G/B	Em9		
C		G/B	D/A	
G5	Em7	G5	Em7	
C	D	G	D	
G*	C* D*	Em**	C**	
D**		Em**		
C**		D**		

Verse 5

G   Em
Maybe there is a God above,

G   Em
But all I've ever learned ___ from love

  C   D   G/B   D
Was how to shoot somebody who ___ out - drew ya.

      G   C   D
And it's ___ not a cry that you hear at night,

Em   C
And it's not somebody who's ___ seen the light,

  D/A   B7/D♯   Em
It's a cold and it's a broken Halle - lujah.

Chorus 5

  D/A C   Em
Hal - le - lujah, Halle - lujah.

      C   G/B D/A
Halle - lujah, Halle - lu - jah.

      C   Cadd9♯11 G6/D Em7 C
Halle - lujah, _____ Halle - lujah.

G/B C   G/B D
Halle - lujah, Halle - lu.

      C   Em
Halle - lujah, Halle - lujah.

      C   G D Cadd9 G/B Em Em(add2) Em C Em
Halle - lujah, Hallelu   -   jah.

    Cmaj7 D G5/D
Halle - lu - jah.

Hold You in My Arms

Words and Music by
Ray LaMontagne and Ethan Johns

Melody:

When you came to me, __

G   Bm7   Em   D   C/G   Bm

D7   D/A   D7/A   F/C   Am

Intro

‖: G   Bm7 | Em   D | C/G | :‖

Verse 1

    G   Bm
When you came to me,

Em   C/G
With your bad dreams and your fears,

        D7   G   D/A D7/A
Was easy to see you'd been crying.

    G   Bm
Seems like ev'rywhere you turn,

Em   C/G
Catastrophe ____ reigns.

        D7   G   D/A D7/A
But who really profits from the dy - ing?

Chorus 1

Em   G   C/G F/C C/G
I could hold you in my arms.

D/A   D7/A   G D/A D7/A
I could hold you for - ever.

G   Bm   Em F/C C/G
And I could hold you in my arms, whoa, oo.

D/A   D7/A   G D/A D7/A
I could hold you for - ever.

Interlude 1	*Repeat Intro*

Verse 2

    G   **Bm**
  When you kissed my lips

Em   **C/G**
  With my mouth so full of questions,

           D7   **G D/A D7/A**
My worried mind, that you qui - et.

G   **Bm**
  Place your hands on my face,

Em   **C/G**
  Close my eyes ____ and say

          D7
That love is a poor man's food.

G   **D/A D7/A**
  Don't prophesize.

Chorus 2   *Repeat Chorus 1*

String Solo

Am			Bm		
Em			C/G		
	D/A D7/A				

Interlude 2   *Repeat Intro*

Verse 3

G   Bm
So, now we see how it is

Em   C/G
As fist begets ___ the spear.

       D7   G   D/A D7/A
Weapons of war, ___ symptoms ___ of madness.

G   Bm
Don't let your eyes refuse to see.

Em   C/G
Don't let your ears ___ refuse to hear.

       D7   G   D/A D7/A
You ain't nev - er gonna shake this sense ___ of sadness.

Chorus 3

Em G   C/G F/C C/G
I could hold you in my arms.

D/A D7/A   G D/A D7/A
I could hold on for - ever.

G   Bm   Em F/C C/G
And I could hold you in my arms, whoa, oo.

D/A D7/A   G D/A D7/A
I could hold on for - ever.

Outro

|G Bm7 |Em D |C/G | |
                Ah.

|G Bm7 |Em D |C/G | |

| | | | | | ‖

I Will Follow You Into the Dark

Words and Music by
Benjamin Gibbard

Love of __ mine, ____ some-day

(Capo 5th fret)

Am   C   F   Gadd4/B   G5   E   Gadd2   Fm   C/G   G/B

Intro

Am	C	F	C Gadd4/B
Am	C	G5	
Am	C	E	Am Gadd2
F	Fm	C/G	

Verse 1

  C/G   Am
Love of mine, someday you will die,

         F
But I'll be close behind.

            C/G   G5
I'll follow you ____ into the dark.

      C/G   Am
No blinding light or tunnels to gates of white.

            F
Just our hands clasped so tight

        C/G   G5
Waiting for ____ the hint of a spark.

Chorus 1

```
             Am                  C
        If heaven and hell decide

                      F            C  Gadd4/B
        That they both ____ are satisfied,

           Am             C             G5
        Il - luminate the nos ____ on their va - cancy signs.

           Am                   C
        If there's no one beside ____ you

                      E              Am  Gadd2
        When your ____ soul embarks,

            F            Fm              C/G
        Then I'll follow you ____ into the dark.
```

Verse 2

```
           C/G                      Am
        In Cath'lic school, as vicious as Roman rule,

               F                  C/G        G5
        I got my knuckles bruised by a la - dy in black.

           C/G                 Am
        And I held my tongue as she told me,

                       F
        "Son, fear is the heart of love."

           C/G            G5
        So I nev - er went back.
```

Chorus 2   *Repeat Chorus 1*

Verse 3

```
            C/G                      Am                            F
You and me, have seen ev'ry - thing to see from Bangkok to Calgary.

              C/G              G5    C/G
And the soles ____ of your shoes ____ are all worn down.

            Am                     F
The time for sleep is now, but it's nothing to cry about

                 C/G             G5          Am         F
'Cause we'll hold ____ each other soon ____ in the black - est of rooms.
```

Chorus 3

```
    Am            C
If heaven and hell decide

              F         C  Gadd4/B
That they both ____ are satisfied,

    Am             C           G5
Il - luminate the no's ____ on their va - cancy signs.

    Am                C
If there's no one beside ____ you

             E              Am  Gadd2
When your ____ soul embarks,

    F           Fm         C  G/B  Am
Then I'll follow you ____ into the dark.

    F           Fm             C/G
And I'll follow you ____ into the dark.
```

I'd Rather Be with You

Words and Music by
Joshua Ryan Radin

Melody:

Sit-tin' here ___ on this

(Capo 1st fret)

C   Gadd4/B   Am   G   F   G/B   Csus4

Intro
‖: C | Gadd4/B | Am | G   :‖

Verse 1

    C   Gadd4/B   Am   G
Sittin' here ___ on this   lonely dock,

    C   Gadd4/B   Am   G
Watch the rain ___ play on ___ the ocean top.

    C   Gadd4/B   Am   G
All the things ___ I feel I   need to say,

    C   Gadd4/B Am   G
I can't explain ___ in any other way.

Chorus 1

                  F   G
I need to be bold, ___ need to jump in the cold ___ water.

               C   G/B   Am
Need to grow older with a girl like you.

              F   G   Am
Finally see ___ you are nat'rally   the one to make it so eas - y

                                G   F   G
When you showed me the truth. ___ Yeah, ___ yeah.

        C   G/B   Am
I'd rather be ___ with you.

    F   G   C   Gadd4/B Am G
Say you want ___ the same thing too.

Verse 2

```
      C                 Gadd4/B    Am              G
      Now here's the sun ___ come ___ to dry the rain,

      C        Gadd4/B              Am        G
      Warm my ___ shoulders and re - lieve my pain.

      C               Gadd4/B        Am              G
      You're the one ___ thing that I'm ___ missing here.

      C              Gadd4/B     Am      G
      With you beside ___ me I no longer fear.
```

Chorus 2

```
                        F                        G
      I need to be bold, ___ need to jump in the cold ___ water.

                  C         G/B      Am
      Need to grow older with a girl like you.

                  F              G                       Am
      Finally see ___ you are nat'rally    the one to make it so eas - y

                                  G        F         G
      When you showed me the truth. ___ Yeah, ___ yeah, yeah.

            C      G/B        Am
      I'd rather be ___ with you.

      F              G             C
      Say you want ___ the same thing too.
```

Bridge	**F Am**
	I could have saved

G   **C   G/B   F**
So much time ___ for us

Am   **G**
Had I seen the way ___ to get where I am today.

F   **Am**   **G**   **C**
You ___ waited on me for so long.

G/B   **F   Am**   **G**
So now ___   listen to me say...

Chorus 3	**F** **G**
	I need to be bold, ___ need to jump in the cold ___ water.

             C   **G/B**   **Am**
Need to grow older with a girl like you.

            F   **G**   **Am**
Finally see ___ you are nat'rally   the one to make it so eas - y

                   G   **F**   **G**
When you showed me the truth. ___ Yeah, ___ yeah, yeah.

 C   **G/B**   **Am**
I'd rather be ___ with you.

F   **G**   **C**
Say you want ___ the same thing ___ too.

Am   **G**   **C   Csus4   C**
Say you feel the way I do.

If It Makes You Happy

Words and Music by Jeff Trott
and Sheryl Crow

Melody:

I be-long ___ a long

G | Gsus2/4 | G* | G6 | C | Cadd4 | C* | D | Am | Em

Intro

| G   Gsus2/4 | G* G6 G* | G   Gsus2/4 | G* G6 G* |
| G   Gsus2/4 | G* G6 G* | G   Gsus2/4 |

Verse 1

Gsus2/4 G* G6 G*   G   Gsus2/4   G   Gsus2/4 G*
    I be - long ____   a long way from here.

G   Gsus2/4
Put on a poncho, ___ played for mosquitoes

G* G   C Cadd4 C* Cadd4
And drank till I was thirsty again.

C   G   Gsus2/4   G* G   Gsus2/4
  We were search - in'   through thrift store jun - gles.

    G* G   Gsus2/4
Found Ge - ronimo's rifle,   Marilyn's shampoo,

G* G   C
And Benny Goodman's corset and pen.

Pre-Chorus 1

  C   D
  Well, okay, I made this up.

  C   D
I promised you I'd never give up.

Chorus 1

    N.C.   Am   C   G
If it makes you hap - py,   it can't be that bad.

D   Am
  If it makes you hap - py,

C   G   Gsus2/4 G* G6 G*
  Then why the hell are you so ___ sad?

| G   Gsus2/4 |

Verse 2

```
Gsus2/4 G* G6 G*    G  Gsus2/4 G*  G         Gsus2/4
        You get  down, ___     a real  low ___ down.
```

```
G* G              Gsus2/4
You listen to Coltrane,    derail your own train.
```

```
G*  G                        C Cadd4 C* Cadd4
Well, who hasn't been there before?
```

```
C        G   Gsus2/4      G*   G      Gsus2/4
  I come 'round,    around the hard ___ way.
```

```
   G* G                Gsus2/4
Bring you comics in bed, scrape the mold off the bread
```

```
G* G                      C
And serve you French toast again.
```

Pre-Chorus 2

```
C                 D
  Well, okay, I still get stoned.
```

```
   C                 D
I'm not the kind of girl you take home.
```

Chorus 2

```
N.C.          Am
If it makes you hap - py,
```

```
C             G
  It can't be that bad.
```

```
D              Am
  If it makes you hap - py,
```

```
C                        G       Gsus2/4 G Gsus2/4 G
  Then why the hell are you so ___ sad?
```

Chorus 3

```
  Gsus2/4 G     Gsus2/4 D Am
If it makes ___ you ___ hap - py,
```

```
C             G
  It can't be that bad.
```

```
D              Am
  If it makes you hap - py,
```

```
C                        Em    Am
  Then why the hell are you so ___ sad?
```

```
|Em        |        |C       |          |
```

Interlude	|G Gsus2/4| G* G6 G*|G Gsus2/4|

Verse 3

    Gsus2/4 G*   G6   G* G Gsus2/4   G* G Gsus2/4
                We've been far, ___   far away from here.

    G* G   Gsus2/4
      Put on a poncho, ___ played for mosquitoes

    G* G   C
    And ev'rywhere in between.

Pre-Chorus 3

    C   D
      Well, okay, we get along.

      C   D
    So what if right now ev'rything's wrong?

Chorus 4   *Repeat Chorus 2*

Chorus 5

     Gsus2/4 G   Gsus2/4 D Am
    If it makes ____ you _____ hap - py,

    C   G
     It can't be that bad.

    D   Am
     If it makes you hap - py,

    C   G   Gsus2/4 G Gsus2/4 G
     Then why the hell are you so ___ sad?

    |Gsus2/4 G Gsus2/4 D |

Guitar Solo

|Am |C |G |
|D |Am |C |
Oh,   oh.

Outro

|:G   Gsus2/4 | G* :| *Play 3 times*
|G |

Ice Cream

Words and Music by
Sarah McLachlan

Melody:

Your love is bet-ter than ice _

Tuning:
(low to high) E–A–D–G–A–D

(Capo 4th fret)

Gadd9 C6/9 Dadd4/A Dadd4 Em11 Am11 Cadd9 Gadd9/B Am7 Em7

Intro   ‖: Gadd9 │ C6/9   │ Dadd4/A │   :‖ *Play 4 times*
           with vocal ad lib

Verse 1
   C6/9   Dadd4 Em11   C6/9
Your love is better than ice ____ cream,

   Am11   Dadd4 Gadd9   Cadd9
Better than anything else that I tried.

   Am11 Dadd4 Em11   C6/9   Gadd9/B
Your love is better than ice ____ cream.

   Am11   Dadd4   C6/9
Ev'ryone one here knows how to ____ cry and fight.

Chorus 1
         Em11 Dadd4 Am11
And it's a long way   down.

       Em11 Dadd4 Am11
It's a long way _____ down.

       Em11 Dadd4 Am7
It's a long way   down to the place

       Gadd9 C6/9   Dadd4 Em11
Where we   started from.

       Gadd9   Am11 Dadd4/A Dadd4
Do, do, do, do, do, do, do, do, do, yeah.

       Gadd9 C6/9   Dadd4
Do, do, 'n', do, _____ ah, ____ yeah.

Verse 2

C§   Dadd4 Em11   C§
Your   love is   better than choc - 'late,

Am11   Dadd4   Gadd9   Cadd9
Better than anything else that I've tried.

Am11 Dadd4 Em11   C§   Gadd9/B
Oh,   love is   better than choc - 'late.

Am11   Dadd4   Cadd9
Ev'ryone here knows how to fight.

Chorus 2

          Em11   Dadd4 Am11
And it's a long   way   down. 'Kay your turn.

          Em Dadd4 Am7
(Audience: Long way   down,

       Em Dadd4 Am7
It's a long way   down to the place

         Gadd9 C§   Dadd4   Em11
Where we   started from.)

Outro   ‖: C§   │ Dadd4 :‖ *Repeat and fade*
                                     w/voc. ad lib.

If You're Gone

Written by
Rob Thomas

Melody:

I think I've al-read-y lost ___ you,

A D F#m E A/C# Bm G5

Asus2 D⁶₉ Aadd2/C# Bsus4 Esus4 G⁶₉

Intro

‖: A   D │   │F#m   E   D │   :‖

Verse 1

A   D
I think I've already lost you,

F#m   E   D
I think you're already gone.

A   A/C# D
I think I'm finally scared now,

A/C#   Bm   E
You think I'm weak, I think you're wrong.

Verse 2

A   D
I think you're already leaving,

F#m   E   D
Feels like your hand is on the door.

A   A/C#   D
I thought this place was an empire,

A/C#   Bm   E
Now I'm re - laxed, I can't be sure.

Pre-Chorus 1

                          Bm   E
And I think you're so mean, ___ I think we should try.

                    A   D
I think I could need ___ this in my life

    A/C#   Bm   E
And I think I'm scared, I think too ___ much.

    G5
I know it's wrong, it's a problem I'm dealing.

Chorus 1

               Asus2   D$\substack{6\\9}$

If you're gone, ___ maybe it's time to come home.

Aadd2/C$\sharp$ Bsus4   Esus4

  There's an aw - ful lot of breathing room,

              Asus2

But I can hardly move.

                            D$\substack{6\\9}$ Aadd2/C$\sharp$

If you're gone, baby, you need to come home, ___ come ___ home.

           Bsus4

There's a lit - tle bit of something me

Esus4   A   D   F$\sharp$m E D

  In ev'rything in ___ you.

Verse 3

   A   D

  I bet you're hard to get over,

F$\sharp$m   E   D

  I bet the room just won't shine.

   A   A/C$\sharp$ D

  I bet my hands I can stay here

    A/C$\sharp$ Bm   E

And I bet you need more than you mind.

Pre-Chorus 2

                      Bm   E

And I think you're so mean, ___ I think we should try.

                  A   D

I think I could need ___ this in my life.

  A/C$\sharp$ Bm   E

I think I'm just ___ scared that I know too ___ much.

  G5

I can't relate and that's a problem I'm feeling.

Chorus 2

               Asus2   D$\substack{6\\9}$

If you're gone, ___ maybe it's time to come home.

Aadd2/C$\sharp$ Bsus4   Esus4

  There's an aw - ful lot of breathing room,

              Asus2

But I can hardly move.

                            D$\substack{6\\9}$ Aadd2/C$\sharp$

If you're gone, baby, you need to come home, ___ come ___ home.

           Bsus4

There's a lit - tle bit of something me

Esus4

  In ev'rything in,

Interlude |**Bsus4** **Esus4** | |**Asus2** **D§** | **Aadd2/C♯** |
             you.

|**Bsus4** |**Esus4** |**Asus2** | | |

                         Bsus4   **Esus4**
Pre-Chorus 3   I think you're so mean, ____ I think we should try.

                        Asus2   **D§**
I think I could need ____ this in my life

     Aadd2/C♯   **Bsus4**
And I think I'm scared.

              Esus4   **G§**
Do I talk too ____ much? I know it's wrong.

It's a problem I'm dealing.

                      Asus2   **D§**
Chorus 3   If you're gone, ____ maybe it's time to come home.

Aadd2/C♯   **Bsus4**   **Esus4**
   There's an aw - ful lot of breathing room,

                      Asus2
But I can hardly move.

And if you're gone, yeah baby,

                      D§   **Aadd2/C♯**
You need to come home, ____ come ____ home.

                  Bsus4   **Esus4**   **Bm** **E**
There's a lit - tle bit of something me ____ in ev'rything in ____ you.
Bm   **E**   **Bm**
   (Something in ____ me,) Ev'rything in,

                      E   **A**
   (Something in ____ me in…) In you.

The Lazy Song

Words and Music by Bruno Mars,
Ari Levine, Philip Lawrence and
Keinan Warsame

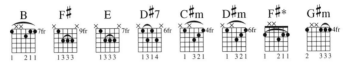

| B | F#| E | D#7 | C#m | D#m | F#* | G#m |

Chorus 1

        B   **F#**   **E**
To - day I don't feel like doin' an - ything.

        B   **F#**   **E**
I just wanna lay in my bed.

           B   **F#**
Don't feel like pickin' up ____ my phone,

           E
So leave a message at the tone

             B   **D#7**   **E**   **N.C.**
'Cause to - day I swear I'm not doin' an - ything. Ah.

Verse 1

           B   **F#**
I'm gonna kick my feet up then stare at the fan,

       E
Turn the TV on, throw my hand in my pants.

       B   **F#**   **E**
Nobody's goin' tell me I can't, ___ no.

          B   **F#**
I'll be loungin' on the couch just chillin' in my Snuggie,

       E
Click to MTV so they can teach me how to dougie.

         B   **F#**   **E**
'Cause in my castle, I'm the frickin' ___ man.

Pre-Chorus 1

        C#m   D#m
Oh, yes, I said it,   I said it.

   E   F#
I said it 'cause I can.

Chorus 2

   B   F#   E
To - day I don't feel like doin' an - ything.

   B   F#   E
I just wanna lay in my bed.

      B   F#
Don't feel like pickin' up ___ my phone,

   E
So leave a message at the tone

        B   D#7   E   N.C.
'Cause to - day I swear I'm not doin' an - ything, noth - in' at all.

Interlude

  B   F#   E   B
(Woo, hoo,   woo, hoo, hoo.) Nothin' at all.

        F#   E
(Woo, hoo,   woo, hoo, hoo.)

Verse 2

        B   F#
Tomorrow I'll wake up, do some P-Ninety-X,

   E
Meet a really nice girl, have some really nice sex.

   B   F#   E
And she's gonna scream out, "This is great!" ___

(Oh my God, this is great.)

        B   F#
Yeah, I might mess around and get my college degree.

  E
I bet my old man will be so proud of me.

   B   F#   E
But sorry, Pops, you'll just have to wait.

Pre-Chorus 2   *Repeat Pre-Chorus 1*

Chorus 3

|B   F#   E|

B   F#   E
To - day I don't feel like doin' an - ything.

B   F#   E
I just wanna lay in my bed.

    B   F#
Don't feel like pickin' up ___ my phone,

    E
So leave a message at the tone

          B   D#7   E
'Cause to - day I swear I'm not doin' an - ything.

Bridge

N.C.   C#m   F#*
    No, I ain't gonna comb my hair

    G#m
'Cause I ain't goin' anywhere,

C#m   F#*   G#m
No, no, no, no, no, no, no, no, no, oh.

      C#m   F#*
I'll just strut in my birthday suit

    G#m
And let ev'rything hang loose,

C#m   F#*   G#m
Yeah, yeah, yeah, yeah, yeah, yeah, yeah, yeah, yeah, yeah.

Chorus 4

N.C.   B   F#   E
    Oh, to - day I don't feel like doin' an - ything.

B   F#   E
I just wanna lay in my bed.

    B   F#
Don't feel like pickin' up ___ my phone,

    E
So leave a message at the tone

          B   D#7   E   N.C.
'Cause to - day I swear I'm not doin' an - ything, noth - in' at all.

Outro

B   F#   E   B
    (Woo, hoo,   woo, hoo, hoo.) Nothin' at all.

          F#   E   N.C.
(Woo, hoo,   woo, hoo, hoo.) Nothin' at all.

Jealousy

Words and Music by
Natalie Merchant

Melody:

Ooh, _____

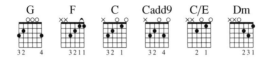

G   F   C   Cadd9   C/E   Dm

Chorus 1

    G   F   C Cadd9 C Cadd9 C
Ooh, ___ jealousy.

    G   F   C Cadd9 C
Ooh, ___ jealousy.

Verse 1

            F   C/E
Is she ___ fine, so well ___ bred,

        Dm   C
The perfect girl, a social ___ deb?

            F   C/E
Is she the sort, you've always ___ thought,

      Dm   C
Could make you what you're ___ not?

Chorus 2   *Repeat Chorus 1*

Verse 2

F   C/E
Is she ___ bright, so well ___ read,

  Dm   C
Are there novels by her ___ bed?

   F   C/E
Is she the sort that you've always ___ said,

  Dm   C
Could satisfy your ___ head?

Chorus 3

G F   C Cadd9 C
 La, la, la, ooh, la, la, la, la, jealousy.

       G   F   C Cadd9 C Cadd9 C
La, la, la, la, la, la, ___ la. Ooh, ___ jealousy.

G   F   C Cadd9 C
 Ooh, ___my jealousy.

Verse 3

    F   C/E
Does she ___ talk the way I ___ do,

  Dm   C
Is her voice reminding ___ you

     F   C/E
Of the promis - es, the little white lies ___ too.

   Dm   C   F
Some - times, tell me while she's touching you,

     C/E Dm   C
Just by mis - take, accident'lly do you say my name?

Jumper

Words and Music by
Stephan Jenkins

Melody:

I wish you would step back from _ that ledge, _ my friend.

Fmaj7   C   Cadd9   G   Am   Dadd$^4_9$ F

Chorus 1

     Fmaj7   **C**   **Cadd9**
I wish you would step back

       G
From that ledge, ___ my friend.

      Fmaj7   **C Cadd9**
You could   cut ties with all the lies

      G
That you've ___ been living in.

   Fmaj7   **C**   **Cadd9**   **G**
And   if you do not want ___ to see me ___ again,

  N.C.   **Fmaj7 C Cadd9 G**
I would under-stand,

      Fmaj7 C Cadd9 G
I would under-stand.

Verse 1

Am
The angry boy, a bit too insane,

C
Icing over a secret pain.

G
You know you don't belong.

Am
You're the first to fight, you're way too loud.

C
You're the flash of light on a burial shroud.

G
I know something's wrong.

Am   Dadd $\frac{4}{9}$
Well, ev'ryone I know has got a rea - son

C   N.C.
To say ___ put the past away.

Chorus 2   *Repeat Chorus 1*

Verse 2

Am
Well, he's on the table and he's gone to code

C   G
And I do not think anyone knows what they are doing here.

Am
And your friends have left you, you've been dismissed.

C
I never thought it would come to this and I,

G
I want you to know

Am   Dadd $\frac{4}{9}$
Ev'ryone's got to face down the de - mons.

C   N.C.
Maybe today, ___ you could put the past away.

Chorus 3

Fmaj7   C   Cadd9
I wish you would step back

               G
From that ledge, ___ my friend.

        Fmaj7   C Cadd9
You could   cut ties with all the lies

               G
That you've ___ been living in.

      Fmaj7   C   Cadd9   G
And   if you do not want ___ to see me ___ again,

  N.C.   Fmaj7 C Cadd9 G
I would under-stand,

            Fmaj7 C Cadd9 G
I would under-stand,

            Fmaj7   C Cadd9 G
I would under - stand.

Guitar Solo

| F   C | G | F   C | G |
                                                   I would understand.

| F   C | G | F   C | G |
                   I would understand.   Understand.

| F   C | G | F   C | G |

| Fmaj7 C | G | Fmaj7 C |

‖: G | Fmaj7   C Cadd9 :‖ *Play 4 times*

| G | Dadd$_9^4$ | C   N.C. |
                                      Can you put the past away?

Chorus 4

Fmaj7   C   Cadd9
I wish you would step back

G
From that ledge, ___ my friend.

Fmaj7
I would understand.

C   Cadd9   G
(I wish you would step back ___ from that ledge, ___ my friend.)

Fmaj7
I would understand.

C   Cadd9   G
(I wish you would step back ___ from that ledge, ___ my friend.)

Fmaj7
And I would under-stand.

C   Cadd9   G
(I wish you would step back ___ from that ledge, ___ my friend.)

Fmaj7
I would under-stand.

C   Cadd9   G
(I wish you would step back ___ from that ledge, ___ my friend.)

Fmaj7   C Cadd9   G
And I would under - stand.

Outro   ‖:Fmaj7 C |G   :‖ *Play 4 times*

Least Complicated

Words and Music by
Emily Saliers

Melody:

I sit two sto-ries a-bove

A   Bm7   Aadd2   D$^6_9$ E   D   A/C#

Bm   F#m   C#m   D5/C#   D5/B   D/F#   Esus4

Intro | A | | | |

Verse 1
         A
I sit two stories above the street.

It's awful quiet here since love fell asleep.

                   Bm7   **Aadd2**
There's life down below me though,

D$^6_9$ **E**   **A**
The kids are walking home from school.

Verse 2
            A
Some long a-go when we were taught

For whatever kind of puzzle you got,

                  Bm7
You just stick the right for-mula in,

Aadd2 **D$^6_9$**   **E**   **A**
A solu-tion for ev-'ry fool.

Pre-Chorus 1
      A   **E**   **D**
  I remember the time ___ when I came so close ___ to you,

          A   **Bm7**
Sent me skipping my class and run-nin' from school.

        D   **E**
And I bought you that ring 'cause I never was cool.

Chorus 1

                       A   **E**   **D**
What makes me think   I could start ____ clean slat - ed?

                    E   **A**
The hardest to learn ____ was the least complicat - ed. Yeah.

Verse 3

              A
Oh, I just sit up in this house and resist

And not be seen until I cease to exist,

                          Bm7   **A/C#**
A kind of conscientious ob - jection,

D⁶   **E**   **A**
  A kind of dodging the draft.

Verse 4

                A
And the boy and girl are holding hands on the street

And I don't want to but I think you just wait.

                    Bm7
It's more than just eye to eye,

A/C#   **D⁶**   **E**   **A**
  Learn the things ____ I could never ____ apply.

Pre-Chorus 2

                                E   **D**
But I remember the time ____ when I came so close with you,

             A   **Bm7**
I let ev'rything go, it seemed the only truth.

             D   **E**
And I bought you that ring, it seemed the thing to do.

Chorus 2

                       A   **E**   **D**
What makes me think   I could start ____ clean slat - ed?

                    E   **A**
The hardest to learn ____ was the least complicat - ed.

                              E   **D**
So what makes me think I could start ____ clean slat - ed?

                    E   **A**
The hardest to learn ____ was the least compli - cated. Oh.

Bridge

    Bm   F#m
I'm just a mirror of a mirror of myself,

  D   E   A
All the things ___ that I do.

      F#m   C#m
And the next time I fall, I'm gonna have to recall

           D   D5/C# D5/B D/F# E   Esus4 E
It isn't love, ___ it's only   some - thing new.

Verse 5   *Repeat Verse 1*

Pre-Chorus 3   A   E   D
  And I remember the time ___ when I came so close ___ with you,

       A   Bm7
Sent me skipping my class and run - nin' from school.

      D   E
And I bought you that ring 'cause I never was cool.

Chorus 3   A   E   D
What makes me think   I could start ___ clean slat - ed?

                    E   A
The hardest to learn ___ was the least complicat - ed.

                         E   D
So, what makes me think I could start ___ clean slat - ed?

                    E   A
The hardest to learn ___ was the least complicat - ed.

(Na, na, na, na, na, na, na.) The least complicated.

(Na, na, na, na, na, na, na.) The least complicated.

Outro   N.C.(A)
‖: (Na, na, na, na, na, na, na.) :‖ *Repeat and fade*

Lucky

Words and Music by Jason Mraz,
Colbie Caillat and Timothy Fagan

Melody:

'N' do you hear me

C   Am   Dm7   G   E7   Am*   Asus4   G13   G7   G#(b5)

Gadd4/B   Gsus4   Em   G*   Dm9   Am7   Dm7*   Am7*   G7/B

Intro | C | |

Verse 1

                          C   **Am**
Jason Mraz: 'N' do you hear me talking to you

             Dm7   **G**   **E7**
Across the water, across the deep blue ocean,

             Am*
Under the open sky?

             Dm7   **G**
Oh, my ____ 'n' baby, I'm try - ing.

                       C   **Asus4 Am**
Colbie Caillat: Mm, boy, I hear you in my dreams.

             Dm7   **G13**
I feel your whisper across the sea.

G7   **E7**   **Am***
   I keep you with me in my heart.

             Dm7   **G**   **G#(b5)**
You make it easier when life gets hard.

Chorus 1

           Am*   **Dm7**   **G**
Both: Lucky I'm in ____ love with my best friend,

                 C   **Gadd4/B Am**
Lucky to have ____ been where I have been.

             Dm7   **Gsus4 G**
Lucky to be coming home a - gain.

	C Am Em G*
Interlude	*Both:* Oo, ___ oo.

	Dm9 Am7 G
Bridge	*Colbie Caillat:* They don't know how long it takes,
	Jason Mraz: They don't know how long it takes,

Dm7*

Both: Waiting for a love like this.

Dm9 Dm7* Dm9 Am7   G

Colbie Caillat: Ev - 'ry   time   we   say goodbye,

Jason Mraz: Ev   -   'ry   time we say good - bye,

Dm7*

Both: I wish we had one more kiss.

Dm9   Am7   G Am7* G7/B

I'll wait for you, I promise you I will.

	Am* Dm7 G
Chorus 2	*Both:* I'm ___ lucky I'm in ___ love with my best friend,

C   Gadd4/B Am

Lucky to have ___ been where I have been.

Dm7   Gsus4 G

Lucky to be coming home a - gain.

Am*   Dm7   G

  Lucky we're in ___ love in ev'ry way,

C   Gadd4/B   Am

Lucky to have ___ stayed where we have stayed.

Dm7   Gsus4 G

Lucky to be coming home some - day.

		C Am

Verse 2

                                  C   Am
Jason Mraz: And so I'm sailing through the ____ sea

          Dm7   G
To an island where we'll meet.

                E7   Am*
You'll hear the music fill the air;

             Dm7 G
I'll put a flower in your hair.

                                C   Asus4 Am
Colbie Caillat: Though the breezes through the trees

          Dm7   G13
Move so pretty, you're all I see.

G7   E7   Am*
  As the world keeps spinning 'round,

       Dm7   G   G#(b5)
You hold me right here, right now.

Chorus 3   *Repeat Chorus 2*

                      C Am Em G*
Outro   Oo, ____ oo.

                      C Am Em
                      Oo, ____ oo.

                      G* C
                      Oo.

Let Him Fly

Words and Music by
Patty Griffin

Melody:

Ain't no talk-ing to this _ man, _____

Drop D tuning:
(low to high) D–A–D–G–B–E

D   G   A   D/A   Bm   Bm7   Em7   F#m7

Intro

| D | | | |
| G | | | |

Verse 1

   G   D
Ain't no talking to this man, ain't no pretty other side.

                G
Ain't no way ____ to understand the stupid words of pride.

               A   D/A   A   G
It would take ____ an acrobat ____ and I ____ already tried all that

          A   D G   D
So   I'm gonna let him fly,   gonna let him fly.

Verse 2

                   D
And things can move ____ at such a pace.

The second hand just waved goodbye.

               G
You know the light ____ has left his face,

But you can't recall just where or why.

             A D/A   A
So there was real - ly nothing to it. ____

D/A   G   A
  I just went and cut ____ right through it.

                  D   G   D
I said I'm gonna let him ____ fly. ____ Oo, yeah, yeah, yeah.

Bridge

           G   **A**
There's no mercy in a live ____ wire,

      Bm   **A Bm Bm7**   **G**
No rest at all in freedom _____ of choic - es we are given.

      Em7   **Bm7**   **A Bm**   **Bm7**
It's ____ a, no choice ____ at all.   Oh,   huh.

      G   **A D**   **Bm**   **F#m7**
The proof is in the fire _____ you touch before it moves a-way,   yeah,

Em7   **A**   **D A**
   But you must always know how long to stay and when to go.

Verse 3

A   **D**
And there ain't no talking to this man. He's been trying to tell me so.

         G   **Bm**
Took awhile ____ to understand the beauty of just   letting go.

                G   **Em7**
'Cause it would take ____ an acrobat and I already tried all that

    A   **D**   **G D**
So   I'm gonna let him ____ fly.

Outro

G   **D G**   **D G**   **D G**
I'm gonna let him fly, fly. Whoa, ____ I'm gonna let him fly, fly.

     D   **G**   **D**
Oh, ____ I'm, ____ I'm gonna let him fly.

Little Lies

Words and Music by
Dave Barnes

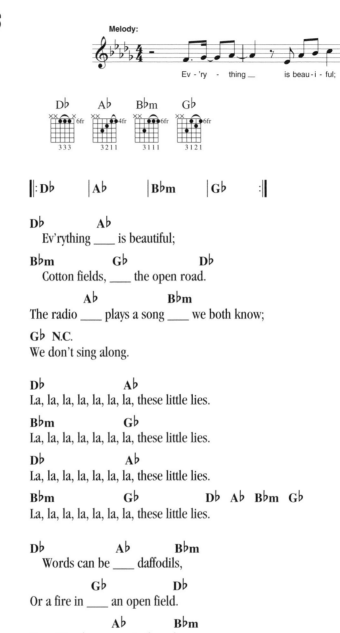

Intro

‖: Db | Ab | Bbm | Gb :‖

Verse 1

Db   Ab
Ev'rything ____ is beautiful;

Bbm   Gb   Db
Cotton fields, ____ the open road.

         Ab   Bbm
The radio ____ plays a song ____ we both know;

Gb N.C.
We don't sing along.

Chorus 1

Db   Ab
La, la, la, la, la, la, la, these little lies.

Bbm   Gb
La, la, la, la, la, la, la, these little lies.

Db   Ab
La, la, la, la, la, la, la, these little lies.

Bbm   Gb   Db Ab Bbm Gb
La, la, la, la, la, la, la, these little lies.

Verse 2

Db   Ab   Bbm
Words can be ____ daffodils,

        Gb   Db
Or a fire in ____ an open field.

        Ab   Bbm
I'm sitting here ____ in the ash

      Gb N.C.
Of stupid words I can't take back.

Chorus 2

D♭   A♭
La, la, la, la, la, la, la, these little lies.

B♭m   G♭
La, la, la, la, la, la, la, these little lies.

D♭   A♭
La, la, la, la, la, la, la, these little lies.

B♭m   G♭
La, la, la, la, la, la, la, these little lies.

Bridge

A♭   D♭   G♭   D♭
  There's a dev - il on my shoulder, ba - by, ooh,

A♭   D♭   G♭   D♭
  And I believe ___ too many things he says, ___ yeah, yeah, yeah.

A♭   D♭   G♭
  I'm fighting these fears as I find the truth,

      A♭ N.C.
And I'm sorry for hurting you.

Interlude   ‖: D♭ | A♭ | B♭m | G♭   :‖

Chorus 3   *Repeat Chorus 2*

Outro-Chorus

D♭   A♭
La, la, la, la, la, la, la, these little lies.

B♭m   G♭
La, la, la, la, la, la, la, these little lies.

D♭   A♭
La, la, la, la, la, la, la, these little lies.

B♭m   G♭ N.C.
La, la, la, la, la, la, la,   these little lies.

Meet Virginia

Words and Music by Pat Monahan,
James Stafford and Rob Hotchkiss

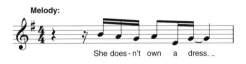

Melody:

She does-n't own a dress.

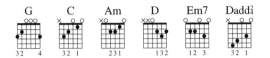

G   C   Am   D   Em7   Dadd$\frac{9}{4}$

Verse 1

      G   **C**
She doesn't own a dress.

Am   **D**
Her hair is al - ways messy.

      G   **C**
You catch her stealin', she won't confess.

Am   **D**
She's beautiful.

G   **C**
Smokes a pack a day.

          Am   **D**
Wait, ____ that's me, but an - yway.

G   **C**
She doesn't care a thing a - bout that hair.

Am   **D**
She thinks I'm beautiful.

G   **C**   **Am D G C Am D**
Meet Virgin - ia.

Verse 2

```
        G              C
     She never com - promises.

Am                D
  Loves babies and ___ surprises.

        G                  C
Wears ___ high heels when she exercises.

Am               D
  Ain't that beau - tiful?

G          C      Am   D
  Meet Virgin - ia.
```

Chorus 1

```
Em7              C       Dadd⁴     Em7
  Well, she wants ___ to be ___ the queen

                C       Dadd⁴      Em7
And she thinks ___ about ___ her scene.

                C       Dadd⁴          Em7
Pulls her hair ___ back as ___ she screams,

                C          Dadd⁴
"I don't real - ly wanna be the queen."
```

Verse 3

```
G                 C
  Daddy wrestles ___ alligators.

Am               D
  Mama works on carburetors.

G                    C
  And brother is a fine

        Am        D
Media - tor for the President.

G                 C              Am
  Well, here she is ___ again on the phone;

               D                  G
Just like me, ___ hates to be alone.

            C              Am              D
We just like to sit at home     and rip on the President.

G          C   Am        D
  Meet Virgin - ia.    Alright.
```

Chorus 2

Em7   C   Dadd$^2_4$ Em7
Well, she wants ____ to live ____ her life.

               C   Dadd$^2_4$ Em7
Then she thinks ____ about ____ her life.

                  C   Dadd$^2_4$ Em7
Pulls her hair ____ back as ____ she screams,

                C   Dadd$^2_4$
"I don't real - ly wanna live ____ this life."

Guitar Solo

‖: Em7 |C |Em7 |C   :‖

Interlude

|G   C |Am D |G   C |Am D |

Verse 4

G   C   Am
She only drinks coffee at mid - night,

          D   G
When the moment is not ____ right.

C   Am   D
Her timing is quite ____ un - usual.

G   C   Am
You see, her confidence is tra - gic,

          D   G
But her intuition mag - ic,

C   Am   D
And the shape of her bod - y, un - usual.

G
Well, meet Virginia.

               N.C.
I can't wait to   meet Virginia.

Yeah, yeah. Hey, hey, hey.

Chorus 3

Em7   C   Dadd$\frac{2}{4}$ Em7
Well, she wants ____ to be ____ the queen

              C   Dadd$\frac{2}{4}$ Em7
And she thinks ____ about ____ her scenes.

              C   Dadd$\frac{2}{4}$ Em7
Well, she wants ____ to live ____ her life.

              C   Dadd$\frac{2}{4}$ Em7
Then she thinks ____ about ____ her life.

            C   Dadd$\frac{2}{4}$ Em7
Pulls her hair ____ back as ____ she screams,

            C   Dadd$\frac{2}{4}$
"I don't real - ly wanna be the queen.

    Em7   C   Dadd$\frac{2}{4}$
‖: Ah, ____ I don't real - ly wanna be the queen. :‖

    Em7   C   Dadd$\frac{2}{4}$
Ah, ____ I don't real - ly wanna live like this."

Name

Words and Music by
John Rzeznik

Melody:

And e - ven though the mo - ment

Tuning:
(low to high) D-A-E-A-E♭-E

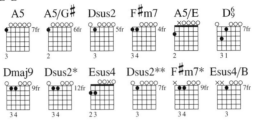

| A5 | A5/G♯ | Dsus2 | F♯m7 | A5/E | D⁶₉ |

| Dmaj9 | Dsus2* | Esus4 | Dsus2** | F♯m7* | Esus4/B |

Intro

‖: A5　　│A5/G♯　│Dsus2　　　│F♯m7 A5/E │
│D⁶₉ Dmaj9 │Dsus2*　│ D⁶₉ Dmaj9 │D⁶₉　　　　:‖

Verse 1

　　　A5　　　　　A5/G♯　　　　　Dsus2
And even though the mo - ment passed me by,

　F♯m7　　　A5/E　　D⁶₉ Dmaj9 Dsus2* D⁶₉ Dmaj9 D⁶₉
I still can't turn ____ away.

　　　A5　　　　　　A5/G♯　　　　　Dsus2
'Cause all the dreams you nev - er thought you'd lose

　F♯m7　　　A5/E　　D⁶₉ Dmaj9 Dsus2* D⁶₉ Dmaj9 D⁶₉
Got tossed along ____ the way.

　　　A5　　　　　A5/G♯　　　　Dsus2
And letters that you nev - er meant to send,

　F♯m7　　　A5/E　　D⁶₉ Dmaj9 Dsus2* D⁶₉ Dmaj9 D⁶₉
Get lost or thrown ____ away.

Chorus 1

F#m7   Esus4   Dsus2
And now we're grown up or - phans that never knew their names.

F#m7   Esus4   Dsus2
We don't belong to no ____ one, that's a shame.

F#m7   Esus4   Dsus2**
You could hide beside ____ me maybe for awhile.

F#m7   Esus4   Dsus2
And I won't tell no ____ one your ____ name.

                        A5   A5/G# Dsus2 F#m7 A5/E
And I won't tell 'em your name.

|D§ Dmaj9 |Dsus2* | D§ Dmaj9 |D§ |

Verse 2

A5   A5/G#   Dsus2
And scars are souvenirs ____ you never lose,

F#m7   A5/E D§ Dmaj9 Dsus2* D§ Dmaj9 D§
The past is nev - er far.

A5   A5/G#   Dsus2
And did you lose yourself ____ somewhere out there,

F#m7   A5/E   D§ Dmaj9 Dsus2* D§ Dmaj9 D§
Did you get to be ____ a star?

A5   A5/G#   Dsus2
And don't it make you sad ____ to know that life

F#m7   A5/E   D§ Dmaj9 Dsus2* D§ Dmaj9 D§
Is more than who ____ we are?

Chorus 2

F#m7   Esus4   Dsus2
We grew up way too fast ____ and now there's nothin' to believe.

 F#m7   Esus4   Dsus2
And reruns all become ____ our history.

 F#m7   Esus4   Dsus2**
A tired song keeps play - in' on a ti - red radio.

 F#m7   Esus4   Dsus2
And I won't tell no ____ one your ____ name.

          A5   A5/G# Dsus2
And I won't tell 'em your name.

F#m7   A5/E   D§ Dmaj9 Dsus2* D§ Dmaj9 D§
I won't tell 'em your name.

A5 A5/G#   Dsus2
Mmm, mmm, mmm.

F#m7   A5/E   D§ Dmaj9 Dsus2* D§ Dmaj9 D§
I won't tell 'em your name.   *Ow!*

Guitar Solo ‖: F#m7 |Esus4 |Dsus2 | :‖ *Play 6 times*

       | |

Verse 3

A5   A5/G#   Dsus2
 I think about ____ you all the time,

 F#m7   A/E   D§ Dmaj9 Dsus2* D§ Dmaj9 D§
But I don't need ____ the same.

 A5   A5/G#   Dsus2
It's lonely where you are. ____ Come back down,

 F#m7   A5/E   Dsus2 F#m7* Esus4/B A5
And I won't tell 'em your name.

Put Your Records On

Words and Music by John Beck,
Steven Chrisanthou and
Corinne Bailey Rae

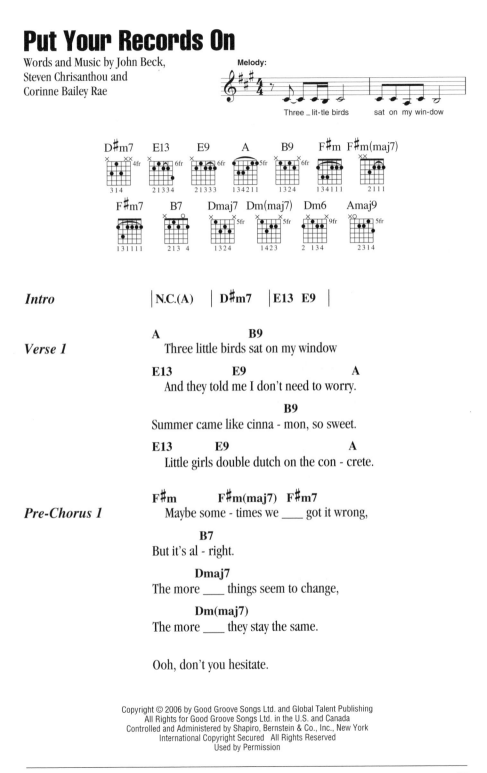

Intro

| N.C.(A) | D#m7 | E13 E9 |

Verse 1

A   **B9**
Three little birds sat on my window

E13   **E9**   **A**
And they told me I don't need to worry.

                              B9
Summer came like cinna - mon, so sweet.

E13   **E9**   **A**
Little girls double dutch on the con - crete.

Pre-Chorus 1

F#m   **F#m(maj7)   F#m7**
Maybe some - times we ____ got it wrong,

        B7
But it's al - right.

        Dmaj7
The more ____ things seem to change,

        Dm(maj7)
The more ____ they stay the same.

Ooh, don't you hesitate.

	A B9
Chorus 1	Girl, put your records on. ___ Tell me your fav'rite song.

E13   E9   A
You go ahead, let your hair ___ down.

                            B9
Sapphire and faded jeans, ___ I hope you get your dreams.

E13   E9   A
Just go ahead, let your hair ___ down.

Dmaj7   Dm6   N.C.(A)
You're gonna find yourself some - where, somehow.

                A   B9
Verse 2   Blue as the sky, sunburnt and lonely,

E13   E9   A
Sippin' tea in a bar by the roadside.

                            B9
Don't you let those other boys ___ fool you,

E13   E9   A
Gotta love that Afro hairdo.

                F♯m   F♯m(maj7) F♯m7
Pre-Chorus 2   Maybe some - times we ___ feel afraid,

                B7
But it's al - right.

                Dmaj7   Dm(maj7)
The more ___ you stay the same, the more ___ they seem to change.

Don't you think it strange?

                A   B9
Chorus 2   Girl, put your records on. ___ Tell me your fav'rite song.

E13   E9   A
You go ahead, let your hair ___ down.

                            B9
Sapphire and faded jeans, ___ I hope you get your dreams.

E13   E9   A
Just go ahead, let your hair ___ down.

Dmaj7   Dm6
You're gonna find yourself some - where, somehow.

Bridge

Bm7
'Twas more than I could take, pity for pity's sake.

F#m7   **N.C.**
Some nights kept me awake, I thought that I was stronger.

Bm7   **Dmaj7 Bm7**
When you gonna realize that you don't even have to try any   longer?

Dmaj7
Do what you want to.

Chorus 3

N.C.   **B9**
Girl, put your records on. ___ Tell me your fav'rite song.

E13   **E9**   **A**
You go ahead, let your hair ___ down.

                              B9
Sapphire and faded jeans, ___ I hope you get your dreams.

E13   **E9**   **A**
Just go ahead, let your hair ___ down.

Outro-Chorus

A   **B9**
Girl, put your records on. ___ Tell me your fav'rite song.

E13   **E9**   **A**
You go ahead, let your hair ___ down.

                              B9
Sapphire and faded jeans, ___ I hope you get your dreams.

E13   **E9**   **A**
Just go ahead, let your hair ___ down.

   Dmaj7   **Dm(maj7)**   **Amaj9**
Ooh, ___ you're gonna find yourself some - where, somehow.

One of Us

Words and Music by
Eric Bazilian

Melody:

If God had a name, _

(Capo 2nd fret)

Em	Csus2	G	D5	Em*	C	D	Dsus4

Intro

‖: **Em Csus2** | **G   D5** :‖ *Play 8 times*

Verse 1

     Em*   **C**
If God had a name,

G   **D5**
   What would it be?

        Em*   **C**
And would you call it to His face

G   **D5**
   If you were faced with Him

   Em* **C**
In all His glory?

G   **D5**
   What would you ask

       Em*   **C**   **G D5**
If you had just one question?

Pre-Chorus 1

   C   Csus2 D
And yeah, yeah,   God is great.

C   Csus2 D5
Yeah, yeah,   God is good.

C   Csus2 Dsus4   D
Yeah, yeah,   yeah, yeah, ____ yeah.

Chorus 1

    Em   Csus2
What if God was one of us,

G D5   Em   Csus2
    Just a slob like one of us,

G D5   Em   Csus2
    Just a stranger on the bus

G   D5   Em   Csus2 G D5
    Try'n' to make His way ___ home?

Verse 2

   Em*   C
If God had a face,

G   D5
    What would it look like?

      Em*   C
And would you want to see

G   D5
    If seeing meant that you would

Em*   C
Have to believe

G   D5
    In things like heaven

     Em*   C
And in Jesus and the saints

    G   D5
And all the proph - ets?

Pre-Chorus 2   *Repeat Pre-Chorus 1*

Chorus 2

      Em   **Csus2**
What if God was one of us,

G D5   **Em**   **Csus2**
    Just a slob like one of us,

G D5   **Em**   **Csus2**
    Just a stranger on the bus

G   **D5**   **Em**   **Csus2**
    Try'n' to make His way ___ home?

G   **D5**   **Em**   **Csus2**
    He's try'n' to make His way ___ home,

G   **D5**   **Em Csus2**
    Back up to heaven all a - lone.

G   **D5**   **Em Csus2**
    Nobody calling on the phone,

G   **D5**
    'Cept for the Pope maybe in Rome.

Guitar Solo

| C   Csus2 | D Dsus4 D | C   Csus2 | D5 | |
| Em Csus2 | G   D5 | Em Csus2 | G   D5 | |

C Csus2	D Dsus4 D	C Csus2	D5	
C Csus2	Dsus4 D	Em Csus2	G D5	
Em Csus2	G D5	Em Csus2	G D5	
Em Csus2	G D5	

Pre-Chorus 3

  Csus2   **D5**
And yeah, yeah, God is great.

C   **Csus2 D5**
Yeah, yeah,   God is good.

C   **Csus2 Dsus4**   **D**
Yeah, yeah,   yeah, yeah, ___ yeah.

Chorus 3

        Em   **Csus2**
What if God was one of us,

G D5   **Em**   **Csus2**
   Just a slob like one of us,

G D5   **Em**   **Csus2**
   Just a stranger on the bus

G   **D5**   **Em**   **Csus2**
   Try'n' to make His way ___ home?

G   **D5**   **Em**   **Csus2**
   Just try'n' to make His way ___ home,

G   **D5**   **Em**   **Csus2**
   Like a holy rollin' ___ stone.

G   **D5**   **Em** **Csus2**
   Back up to heaven all a - lone,

G   **D5**   **Csus2**
   Just try'n' to make His way ___ home.

Nobody callin' on the phone,

'Cept for the Pope, maybe, in Rome.

Round Here

Words by Adam Duritz
Music by Dave Janusko, Dan Jewett,
Chris Roldan and David Bryson

Melody:

Step out __ the front door like a ghost __

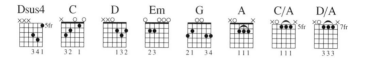
Dsus4 C D Em G A C/A D/A

Intro   ‖: N.C.(Dsus4) | :‖

Verse 1

   N.C.(C)   (D)
   Step out the front door like a ghost ___ into the fog

            (Em)   (G)
   Where no one noti - ces the contrast of white ___ on white.

        (C)   (D)
   And in be - tween the moon and you the an - gels get a better view

            (Em)   (G)
   Of the crumbl - ing difference between wrong ___ and right.

        (C)   (D)
   I walk in the air between the rain, through myself and back again.

        (Em)   (G)   (C)
   Where?   I don't know.   Maria says she's dying.

               (D)   (Em)
   Through the door I hear her crying, "Why?" I don't know.

Chorus 1

   (G)   C   D   Em
   Round here ___ we al - ways stand up straight.

   G   C   D   Em G
   Round here ___ something radiates.

Verse 2

     N.C.(C)   (D)
Maria came from Nashville with a suitcase ___ in her hand.

             (Em)   (G)
She said she'd like ___ to meet a boy who looks like El - vis.

         (C)   (D)
And she walks ___ along the edge of where the o - cean meets the land

           (Em)   (G)
Just like she's walk - ing on a wire in the cir - cus.

         (C)   (D)
She parks her car outside of my house, an'   takes her clothes off,

     (Em)   (G)
Says she's so close to understanding Je - sus.

         (C)   (D)
And she knows she's more than just a little mis - understood.

          (Em)   G
She has trouble acting normal when she's ner - vous.

Chorus 2

               C   D   Em
Round here ___ we're carv - ing out our names.

G   C D   Em
 Round here ___ we all look the same.

G   C   D
 Round here ___ we talk just like li - ons

     Em   G
But we sacrifice like lambs.

        C   D   Em A D
Round ___ here she's slipping through my hands.

Bridge

     A   C/A   D/A   A
Run home. Sleep - ing children better run like ___ the wind.

C/A   D/A   A
Out of the lightning dream.

   C/A   D/A   A
Ma - ma's little baby better get herself ___ in

C   D
Out of the lightning.

Verse 3

   N.C.(C)   (D)   (Em)
   She says, "It's on - ly in my head."

(G)   (C)   (D)   (Em)
  She says, "Shhh…   I know it's on - ly in my head."

(G)   (C)
  But the girl ____ on the car in the parking lot says,

 (D)
"Man, you should try to take a shot."

(Em)   (G)
Can't you see my walls are crum - bling?

        (C)   (D)
Then she looks up at the building says she's think - in' of jumping.

        (Em)   (G)
She says she's tired ____ of life; she must be tired ____ of something.

Chorus 3

        C   D   Em
Round here ____ she's al - ways on my mind.

G   C   D   Em
  Round here, ____ hey, man, I got lots of time.

G   C   D
  Round here we're never sent to bed ear - ly.

     Em   G
Man, no - body makes us wait.

        C   D   Em   G
Round here ____ we stay up ver - y, very, ver - y, very late.

        C   D   Em
I, I can't see no - thin', noth - in' around ____ here.

   G   C   D
Ah, ____ you catch me if I'm fall - in', you catch me if I'm fall - in'.

                 Em   G
Will you catch me 'cause I'm   fallin' down on you?

         N.C.(C)   (D)   (Em)
I said I'm un - der the gun   around ____ here.

(G)   (C)   (D)   (Em)
  Ah, man, I said I'm under the gun ____ around ____ here.

(G)   (C)   (D)   (Em)
  And I can't see nothin',   nothin' ____ around here.

Save Tonight

Words and Music by
Eagle Eye Cherry

Melody:

Go on __ and close   the

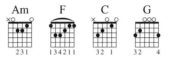

Am   F   C   G

Intro
‖: Am F |C G |Am F |C G :‖

Verse 1

        Am F   C
Go on and close   the curtains,

  G   Am F   C
  'Cause all we need   is can - dlelight.

  G   Am   F   C
  You and ___ me,   and a bottle of wine,

  G   Am   F   C
  Gonna hold you tonight,   ah, yeah.

Verse 2

  G   Am F C   G
  Well, we know   I'm going away,

        Am F   C
And how I wish,   I wish it weren't ___ so.

  G   Am F C   G
  So take this wine,   and drink with me.

Am   F
Let's delay our misery.

Chorus 1

       C G   Am   F   C   G
       Save to - night,   and fight the break of dawn.

           Am   F   C   G
       Come ____ tomorrow,   to - morrow I'll be gone.

           Am   F   C   G
       Save ____ tonight,   and fight the break of dawn.

           Am   F   C   G
       Come ____ tomorrow,   to - morrow I'll be gone.

Verse 3

           Am F   C
       There's a log   on the fire,

       G   Am F   C   G
       And it burns   like me ____ for you.

           Am   F   C G
       Tomorrow comes   with one desire,

          Am   F   C
       To take me a - way, oh, it's true.

Verse 4

       G   Am F   C   G
       It ain't easy ____ to say goodbye.

          Am   F   C   G
       Darlin', please   don't start ____ to cry.

          Am   F   C   G
       'Cause girl, you know I've got to go.   Oh.

          Am   F
       And Lord, I wish it wasn't so.

Chorus 2   *Repeat Chorus 1*

Guitar Solo 1	‖: Am F │C G :‖ *Play 4 times*

            Am   **F** **C**   **G**

Verse 5   To - morrow comes ___ to take me a - way.

Am   **F**   **C**   **G**
  I wish that I, that I could stay.

   Am   **F**   **C** **G**
But girl, you know I've got to go,   oh.

   Am   **F**
And Lord, I wish it wasn't so.

Chorus 3   *Repeat Chorus 1*

Chorus 4

           Am **F**   **C**   **G**
Save to - night,   and fight the break of dawn.

           Am   **F**   **C**   **G**
Come ___ tomorrow,   to - morrow I'll be gone.

          Am   **F**   **C**   **G**
Save ___ tonight,   and fight the break of dawn.

          Am   **F**   **C**   **G**
Come ___ tomorrow,   to - morrow I'll be gone.

    Am F   **C**   **G**
‖:   To - morrow I'll be gone. :‖ *Play 4 times*

Guitar Solo 2   ‖:Am F │C G :‖ *Play 3 times*
│Am   F │

   C G   **Am F**

Outro   ‖:   Save to - night. :‖ *Repeat and fade*

The Scientist

Words and Music by Guy Berryman,
Jon Buckland, Will Champion
and Chris Martin

Melody:

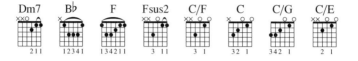
Come up to meet ___ you,

Dm7   B♭   F   Fsus2   C/F   C   C/G   C/E

Intro ‖: **Dm7** | **B♭** | **F** | **Fsus2** :‖

Verse 1

Dm7   **B♭**
   Come up to meet ___ you,

         F
Tell you I'm sor - ry,

              Fsus2
You don't know how love - ly you are.

Dm7   **B♭**
   I had to find ___ you,

         F
Tell you I need ___ you,

         Fsus2   **C/F**
Tell you I'll set ___ you apart.

Dm7   **B♭**
   Tell me your se - crets,

          F
And ask me your ques - tions,

        Fsus2   **C/F**
Oh, let's go back ___ to the start.

Dm7   **B♭**
   Running in cir - cles,

         F
Coming up tails,

        Fsus2   **C/F**
Heads on a silence ___ apart.

Chorus 1

Bb
   Nobody said it was easy,

F   Fsus2
   It's such a shame ____ for us to part.

Bb
   Nobody said it was easy,

F   C/F   Fsus2   C
   No one ever said ____ it would be ____ this hard.

C/G
   Oh, take me back to the start.

Interlude 1

| F | Bb | F | | |
| Dm7 | Bb | F | Fsus2 | |

Verse 2

Dm7   Bb
   I was just guess - ing

             F
At numbers and fig - ures,

Pulling your puzzles apart.

Dm7   Bb
   Questions of sci - ence,

           F
Science and prog - ress,

           Fsus2
Do not speak as loud ____ as my heart.

Dm7   Bb
   Tell me you love ____ me,

           F
Come back and haunt ____ me,

        Fsus2
Oh, and I rush ____ to the start.

Dm7   Bb
   Running in cir - cles,

           F
Chasing our tails,

        Fsus2   C/E
Coming back ____ as we are.

	B♭
Chorus 2	Nobody said it was easy,
	F **Fsus2**
	Oh, it's such a shame ___ for us to part.
	B♭
	Nobody said it was easy,
	F **C/F** **Fsus2** **C**
	No one ever said ___ it would be so ___ hard.
	C/G
	I'm going back to the start.
Interlude 2	|**F** |**B♭** |**F** | |
	|**Dm7** |**B♭** |**F** | |
	Dm7 B♭ F
Outro	Ooh.
	Dm7 B♭ F
	Ah, ooh.
	Dm7 B♭ F
	Oh, ooh.
	Dm7 B♭ F
	Oh, ooh.

She Runs Away

Words and Music by
Duncan Sheik

Melody:

You may not see the end of it,

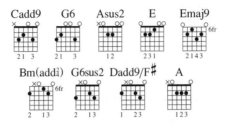

Cadd9 G6 Asus2 E Emaj9

Bm(add♮4) G6sus2 Dadd9/F♯ A

Intro ‖: **Cadd9 G6** |**Asus2 E** :‖

Verse 1
                    Cadd9   G6
You may not see the end of it,

       Asus2   E
But luckily she comes around.

       Cadd9   G6
It isn't what she ____ talks about,

       Asus2   E
It's just the way she ____ is.

Pre-Chorus 1
                              Emaj9   Bm(add♮4)
And she says, "Ooh, Darlin' don't ____ you know

       G6sus2 Dadd9/F♯   **Asus2   A**
The darkness _____ comes and the dark - ness goes?"

              Emaj9   **Bm(add♮4)**
She says, "Ooh, Babe, why don't you ____ let it go?

G6sus2   Dadd9/F♯   **Asus2   A**
Happiness ain't ____ never how you think ____ it should be so."

Verse 2

Cadd9   G6
I mystified the simple life,

  Asus2   E
I covered up with consciousness,

Cadd9   G6
I saw myself and broke it down

   Asus2   E
'Till nothing more was ___ left.

    Cadd9   G6
She saw the symptoms ___ right away

   Asus2   E
And spoke to me in poetry.

      Cadd9   G6
Some - times the more you ___ wonder why,

   Asus2   E
The worse it seems to ___ get.

Pre-Chorus 2   *Repeat Pre-Chorus 1*

Chorus 1

Emaj9   Bm(add¾) G6sus2 Dadd9/F# Asus2 A
 She runs away.

Emaj9   Bm(add¾) G6sus2 Dadd9/F# Asus2 A
 She runs away.

Interlude | Asus2 A | Asus2 A |

Verse 3

      Cadd9   G6
And then, you know there ___ comes a time

      Asus2   E
You need her more than anything.

      Cadd9   G6
You may believe yours ___ are the wounds

      Asus2   E
That only she can ___ heal,

      Cadd9   G6
Then ev'rything will turn around.

Asus2   E
She becomes so serious.

Cadd9   G6
What she chose to ___ offer you

      Asus2   E
Was all that you could have.

Pre-Chorus 3   *Repeat Pre-Chorus 1*

Chorus 2

   Emaj9   Bm(add³₄) G6sus2 Dadd9/F♯ Asus2 A
||: She runs away.   :||

Emaj9   Bm(add³₄) G6sus2 Dadd9/F♯ Asus2 A
 She runs away.   Aah.

Emaj9   Bm(add³₄) G6sus2 Dadd9/F♯ Asus2 A
 She runs away.

6th Avenue Heartache

Words and Music by
Jakob Dylan

Melody:

Si - rens _ ring,   the shots ring out, _

F   C   Gm7   Bb

134211   32 1   131111   1333

Intro
‖: F | C | Gm7 | Bb :‖

Verse 1

      F   C
Sirens ring, the shots ring out,

      Gm7   Bb
A stranger cries, screams out loud.

          F   C
I had my world strapped against my back.

      Gm7   Bb
I held my hands, never knew ____ how to act.

Chorus 1

             F
And the same ____ black line that was drawn on you

   C   Gm7
Was drawn on me, and now it's drawn me in.

      Bb
Sixth Avenue heartache.

Interlude 1
| F | C | Gm7 | Bb |

Verse 2

       F   C
Below me, now was a homeless ___ man

     Gm7   Bb
Singing a songs I knew com - plete.

              F   C
On the steps alone, ___ his guitar in ___ hand,

     Gm7   Bb
It's fifty years stood where he stands.

Chorus 2

                F
‖: And the same ___ black line that was drawn on you

   C   Gm7
Was drawn on me, and now it's drawn me in.

     Bb
Sixth Avenue heartache. :‖

Interlude 2   *Repeat Interlude 1*

Verse 3

       F   C
Walking home on the ___ streets,

     Gm7   Bb
The river winds move my feet.

          F   C
The subway steam, like silhouettes in dreams,

       Gm7   Bb
They stood by me just like moon - beams.

Chorus 3   *Repeat Chorus 1*

Chorus 4

             F
And the same ___ black line that was drawn on you

   C   Gm7
Was drawn on me, and now it's drawn me in.

     Bb
Sixth Avenue heart…

| *Guitar Solo* | | F | C | Gm7 | B♭ | |

Guitar Solo

| | F | C | Gm7 | B♭ | |

Ache.

| | F | C | Gm7 | B♭ | |

Verse 4

               F   C

Looked out the window, and down upon that street,

                 Gm7   B♭

And gone like the midnight was that ____ man.

               F   C

But I see his six strings laid against that wall,

            Gm7   B♭

And all his things, they all look so ____ small.

                   F   C

I've got my fingers ____ crossed on a shooting ____ star.

          Gm7   B♭

Just like me, they just moved ____ on.

Chorus 5

Repeat Chorus 1

Chorus 6

               F

And the same ____ black line that was drawn on you

    C   Gm7

Was drawn on me, and now it's drawn me in.

            B♭   F

Sixth Avenue heartache, heart - ache.

  C   Gm7 B♭

  Now it's drawing me in.   Heartache.

               F

And the same ____ black line that was drawn on you

    C   Gm7

Was drawn on me, and now it's drawn me in.

            B♭   F   C Gm7 B♭

Sixth Avenue heartache, heart - ache.

Outro

Repeat Interlude 1 and fade

The Space Between

Words and Music by
David J. Matthews and Glen Ballard

You can-not quit _ me so quick - ly. ___

Tune down 2 1/2 steps:
(low to high) B-E-A-D-F♯-B

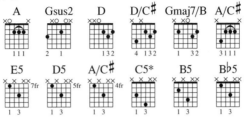

Verse 1

    A Gsus2
        You cannot quit me so quickly.

    A Gsus2
        Is no hope in you for me.

    A Gsus2
        No corner you could squeeze me.

    A Gsus2   A
        But I got all the time for you, love.

Chorus 1

    D   D/C♯   Gmaj7/B
    The space between ___ the tears we cry

                        A/C♯   D
Is the laughter, keeps us coming back for more.

                D/C♯   Gmaj7/B
The space between ___ the wicked lies ___ we tell

                A   Gsus2
And hope to keep us safe from the pain.

          A   Gsus2
But will I hold you a - gain?

Verse 2

Gsus2
These fickle, fuddled words can confuse me,

A Gsus2
Like "Will it rain today?"

A Gsus2
Waste the hours with talking, talking.

A Gsus2   A
These twisted games we're playing.

Chorus 2

D   D/C♯   Gmaj7/B
We're strange al - lies with warring hearts.

                        A/C♯ D
What a wide-eyed beast you ____ be.

                        D/C♯   Gmaj7/B
The space between ____ the wicked lies ____ we tell

                        A   Gsus2
And hope to keep us safe from the pain.

            A   Gsus2   A
But will I hold you a - gain? *Will I* hold...

Bridge

E5   D5   A/C♯*
Look at us spinning out in the ____ madness

            C5   B5
Of a roll - er coast - er.

E5   D5   A/C♯*
You know you went off like a devil in a church,

            C5   B5
In the middle of a crowd - ed room.

E5   D5
All we can do, my love,

A/C♯*   C5   B♭5
Is hope we don't take this ship down.

Chorus 3

    D   D/C♯   Gmaj7/B
The space between ___ where you smile and hide,

                           A/C♯ D
That's where you'll find me if I get to go.

                 D/C♯   Gmaj7/B
The space between ___ the bullets in our fi - refight

                       A/C♯ D
Is where I'll be hiding, waiting for you.

                D/C♯   Gmaj7/B
The rain that falls ___ splashed in your heart,

                      A/C♯   D
Ran like sadness down the window in - to your room.

               D/C♯   Gmaj7/B
The space between ___ our wicked lies

                     A/C♯   D
Is where we hope to keep safe from ___ pain.

            D/C♯   Gmaj7/B A/C♯ D
Take my hand ___ 'cause were walking ___ out of here.

     D/C♯   Gmaj7/B   A/C♯
Oh, oh. Right out of here, ___ love is all we need, dear.

Outro-Chorus

    D   D/C♯   Gmaj7/B
The space between ___ what's wrong and right

                           A/C♯ D
Is where you'll find me hiding, waiting for you.

                 D/C♯   Gmaj7/B
The space between ___ your heart and ___ mind

                     A/C♯
Is the space we'll fill with time.

      D   D/C♯ Gmaj7/B A/C♯
||:   The space between.   :| *Repeat and fade*

Songbird

Words and Music by
Christine McVie

For _____ you _____

G   Cadd9   D   Am7   G/B   Am
Em   C   D7   D7/F♯   G*   C/G

Intro

|G |Cadd9 |G |Cadd9 |
|G |

Verse 1

     G D   Cadd9   G
        For you ____ there'll be ____ no crying.

Am7 G/B   Cadd9
For ____ you

G
    The sun will be shining

Am7 G/B   Am   Em
    'Cause I feel that when I'm with you

     Cadd9   G
It's al - right. I know ____ it's right.

Chorus 1

               D   C
And the song - birds keep singing

            Em
Like they know ____ the score.

           C   D7   D7/F♯
And I love ____ you, I love you, I love you

          G*   C/G G* Am7 G/B
Like never before.

Guitar Solo

Cadd9			G* C/G	G* Am7 G/B
Cadd9			G	
D	C		Em	
C	D7 D7/F♯	G* C/G	G*	

Verse 2

Cadd9   G   C/G
To you I would give the world.

G Am7 G/B Cadd9
  To_____ you

 G
I'd ___ never be cold

Am7 G/B Am   Em
 'Cause ___ I feel that when I'm with you

  Cadd9   G
It's al - right. I know ___ it's right.

Chorus 2

       D   C
And the song - birds keep singing

      Em
Like they know ___ the score.

     C   D7 D7/F♯
And I love ___ you, I love you, I love you

    G Am7 G/B
Like never before.

C   G Am7 G/B
 Like never be - fore.

C   G
 Like never be - fore.

Stay

Words and Music by
Lisa Loeb

(Capo 6th fret)

Gsus2   Em7   A7sus4 Gmaj7/B Csus2   Am7

G   Gsus4   Csus2*   Cm   G5

Intro

|Gsus2 |Em7 |A7sus4 Gmaj7/B |Csus2 |

Verse 1

Gsus2   Em7   A7sus4 Gmaj7/B Csus2
You say   I only hear what I want to.

Gsus2   Em7   A7sus4 Gmaj7/B Csus2
You say   I talk so all the time,   so.

Am7   G
And I thought what I felt was simple,

Am7   G   Gsus4
And I thought that I don't ____ belong.

Am7   G
And now that I am leaving,

Am7   G
Now I know that I did something wrong

        Csus2*   Cm   Am7   G Am7 G
'Cause I missed you.   Yeah, yeah, I missed you.

Verse 2

Gsus2   Em7
And you say   I only hear what I want to.

A7sus4   Gmaj7/B
I don't listen hard, don't pay attention

     Csus2   G5
To the distance that you're running to anyone, anywhere.

A7sus4   Gmaj7/B
I   don't understand ___ if you really care.

  Csus2
I'm only hearing negative. No, no, no.

  Am7   G
So I,   I turned the radi - o on, I turned the radio up,

Am7   G
And this woman was singing my song.

Am7   G
Lovers in love and the others run away,

Am7   G
Lover is crying 'cause the other won't stay.

Am7   G
Some of us hover when we weep for the other

    Am7   G
Who was dying since the day they were born.

    Am7   G
Well, well,   this is not that.

                             Am7   G
I think that I'm throwing, but I'm ___ thrown.

    A7sus4
And I thought I'd live forever, but now I'm not so sure.

    Csus2
You try to tell me that I'm clever,

                       A7sus4   Gmaj7/B Csus2
But that won't take me anyhow ___ or anywhere   with you.

Verse 3

Am7   G
You said that I was naïve,

 Am7   G
And I thought that I was strong, oh.

Am7   G
I thought, "Hey I can leave, I can leave."

 Am7   G
Oh, ____ but now I know that I was wrong

   Csus2* Cm Am7   G
'Cause I missed you. Yeah, ____ I missed you.

Am7 G   A7sus4
   You said, "You caught me 'cause you want me,

And one day you'll let me go."

     Csus2
You try to give away a keeper or keep me

         A7sus4   Gmaj7/B Csus2
'Cause you know you're just so scared to lose.

Outro

     Gsus2 Em7 A7sus4 Gmaj7/B Csus2
And you say,   "Stay."

Gsus2 Em7   A7sus4 Gmaj7/B Csus2
 You say I only hear what I want to.

Sunny Came Home

Words and Music by
Shawn Colvin and John Leventhal

Melody:

Sun-ny came home   to her fav-'rite   room, _

(Capo 2nd fret)

Am*   Asus2   Am   G   F   Em   C   F#m7♭5

Dm9   Dm   Fmaj7#4   Fmaj7   Dm7   D7/F#   G/B

Intro

‖: Am*   Asus2 | Am* Asus2 :‖
| Am   G | F   Em | Am   G | C   G |
| F#m7♭5 G | F   Em | F   G | Dm9 |

Verse 1

Am   G   F   Em
Sunny came home to her fav'rite room.

Am   G   C   G
Sunny sat down in the kitchen.

F#m7♭5   G   F   Em
She opened a book and a box of tools.

Dm   Am   Fmaj7#4   Fmaj7
Sunny came home with a mission.

Chorus 1

                    C   G   Dm7   F
She says, "Days ___ go by, ___ I'm hyp - notized,

          C   G   Dm7
I'm walk - ing on ___ a wire.

          C   G
I close ___ my eyes

          Dm7   Am   D7/F#
And fly   out of ___ my mind

G   Fmaj7
Into the fire."

Interlude 1 |Am   G |F   Em |Am   G |C   G |

Verse 2
           Am   G   C   G
           Sunny came home with a list of names.

           Am   G   C   Em
           She didn't believe ____ in tran - scendence.

           F   G   Am   G
           "It's time for a few small re - pairs," she said,

           Dm7   Am   Fmaj7#4   Fmaj7
           But Sunny came home with a vengeance.

Chorus 2
                    C   G   Dm7   F
           She says, "Days ____ go by, ____ I don't ____ know why

                 C   G   Dm7
           I'm walk - ing on ____ a wire.

                  C   G
           I close ____ my eyes

               Dm7   Am   D7/F#
           And fly   out of ____ my mind

           G   Fmaj7
           Into the fire."

Bridge
                 G/B   Em   F
           Get ____ the kids ____ and bring ____ a sweater.

                 G/B   Em   F
           Dry ____ is good ____ and wind ____ is better.

                 G/B   Em   F
           Count ____ the years ____ you al - ways knew it.

                 G/B   Em   Fmaj7#4   Fmaj7
           Strike ____ a match, ____ go on ____ and do ____ it.

	C **G** **Dm7** **F**
Chorus 3	Oh, days ___ go by, ___ I'm hyp - notized,

                      C   **G**   **Dm7**
I'm walk - ing on ___ a wire.

                C   **G**
I close ___ my eyes

      Dm7   **F**   **C**
And fly   out of ___ my mind

     G   **Dm7**
Into ___ the fire.

            C   **G**   **Dm7**   **F**
Oh, light ___ the sky ___ and hold ___ on tight,

            C   **G**   **Dm7**
The world ___ is burn - ing down.

          C   **G**   **Dm7**
She's out ___ there on ___ her own

         Am   **D7/F♯**
And she's ___ alright.

G   **Fmaj7** **F♯m7♭5** **Am** **D7/F♯**
  Sunny came home.

             Am* **Asus2** **Am*** **Asus2**   **Am*** **Asus2**
Sunny came home.   **Mm.**

Am* **Asus2** **Am*** **Asus2** **Am*** **Asus2** **Am*** **Asus2** **Am*** **Asus2**
    Mm.

Outro	| **Am*** **Asus2** |**Am*** **Asus2** | **Am*** **Asus2** |**Am*** **Asus2** |

              | **Am*** **Asus2** |**Am*** **Asus2** | **A5**

Steal My Kisses

Words and Music by
Ben Harper

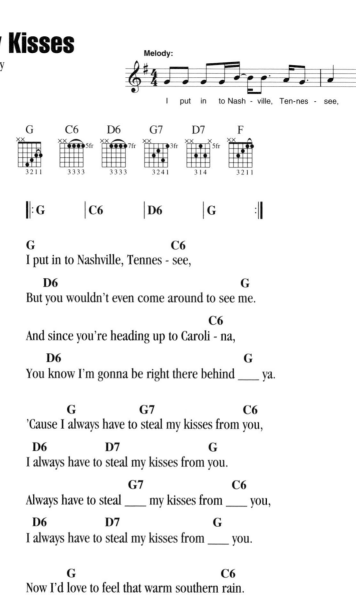

Melody:

I put in to Nash - ville, Ten-nes - see,

G   C6   D6   G7   D7   F

Intro

‖: G |C6 |D6 |G :‖

Verse 1

    G   C6
I put in to Nashville, Tennes - see,

       D6   G
But you wouldn't even come around to see me.

                            C6
And since you're heading up to Caroli - na,

       D6   G
You know I'm gonna be right there behind ____ ya.

Chorus 1

                G   G7   C6
'Cause I always have to steal my kisses from you,

    D6   D7   G
I always have to steal my kisses from you.

                    G7   C6
Always have to steal ____ my kisses from ____ you,

    D6   D7   G
I always have to steal my kisses from ____ you.

Verse 2

              G   C6
Now I'd love to feel that warm southern rain.

       D6   G
Just to hear it fall is the sweetest sounding thing.

                            C6
And to see it fall on your simple country dress,

       D6   G
It's like ____ heaven to me, I must con - fess.

Chorus 2   *Repeat Chorus 1*

Interlude

N.C.						
G F	G F	G F	G F	

Verse 3

        G   **C6**
Now I've been hanging 'round you for days

     D6   **G**
But when I lean in you just turn your head a - way.

                   C6
Whoa, no, you didn't mean that.

               D6   **G**
She said, "I love ____ the way you think, but I hate the way you act."

Chorus 3

          G **N.C.**
'Cause I always have to steal my kisses from you,

I always have to steal my kisses from you.

Always have to steal my kisses from you,

I always have to steal my kisses from you.

G   **G7**   **C6**
Always have to steal ____ my kisses from you,

D6   **D7**   **G**
I always have to steal my kisses from you.

                     G7   **C6**
I always have to steal ____ my kisses from ____ you,

D6   **D7**   **G**
I always have to steal my kisses from ____ you.

Outro   ‖: G | C6 | D6 | G   :‖ *Repeat and fade*

Stolen

Words and Music by
Chris Carrabba

Melody:

We watch the sea-son pull ____

Tune down 1/2 step:
(low to high) Eb-Ab-Db-Gb-Bb-Eb

E   E/A   C#m7   E5   Bsus4   C#m7*   Asus2   B5

C#7sus4   Asus2*   E5*   C#m7**   Asus6/9   Amaj7sus2   E5**

Intro

‖: E | E/A | C#m7 | E/A :‖

Verse 1

E5   Bsus4   C#m7*
We watch the season pull ____ up its own stakes

                              Asus2
And catch the last weekend ____ of the last week.

E5   Bsus4   C#m7*
Before the gold and the glimmer have been replaced,

Another sun soaked season fades away.

Chorus 1

E   E/A   C#m7 E/A
You have stolen my   heart.

E   E/A   C#m7 E/A
You have stolen my   heart.

Verse 2

B5   C#7sus4
Invitation only, grand farewells,

                     Asus2*
Crash the best one   of the best ones.

B5   C#7sus4
Clear liquor and cloudy eyed,

            Asus2*
Too early to ____ say good night.

Chorus 2   *Repeat Chorus 1*

Bridge

E5*   C#m7**   Asus§
And from the ballroom floor ___ we are in celebra - tion.

   Amaj7sus2   E5*
One good stretch before our hi - bernation.

             C#m7**   Asus§   Amaj7sus2
Our dreams assured, ___ and we all ___ will sleep well.

         E   E/A   C#m7
Sleep well. ___   Sleep well.

E/A   E   E/A   C#m7 E/A
  Sleep well. ___   Sleep well.

Outro-Chorus

E   E/A C#m7   E/A
You have stolen,   you have stolen,

E   E/A   C#m7 E/A
  You have stolen my ___ heart.

E   E/A   C#m7
  I watch you spin around ___ in your highest heels.

            E/A   E
You are the best one ___ of the best ones.

     E/A   C#m7 E/A
We all look like we   feel.

E   E/A
  You have stolen my,

C#m7   E/A
  You have stolen my,

E   E/A   C#m7 E/A E5**
  You have stolen my   heart.

Thank You

Words and Music by
Paul Herman and Dido Armstrong

My tea's gone cold, I'm won - d'ring why ___ I

(Capo 4th fret)

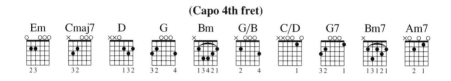

Em   Cmaj7   D   G   Bm   G/B   C/D   G7   Bm7   Am7

Intro ‖: Em   Cmaj7 | Em   Cmaj7 :‖ *Play 4 times*

Verse 1

    Em   Cmaj7   D
My tea's gone cold, I'm wond'ring why

    G   Bm   Em
I got out of bed at all.

            Cmaj7   D
The morning rain ___ clouds up my win - dow

    G   Bm
And I can't see at all,

Em   Cmaj7   D
   And even if ___ I could it'd all ___ be grey,

        G   Bm   Em
But your picture on ___ my wall,

       Cmaj7   Em
It reminds ___ me that it's not so bad,

     Cmaj7   Em Cmaj7 Em Cmaj7
It's not so bad.

Verse 2

    Em   Cmaj7   D
I drank too much ___ last night, got bills to pay.

   G   Bm   Em
My head just feels in pain.

                Cmaj7   D
I missed the bus ___ and there'll be hell today.

   G   Bm   Em
I'm late for work again.

           Cmaj7   D
And even if ___ I'm there they'll all ___ imply

     G   Bm   Em
That I might not last the day,

             Cmaj7   Em
And then you call ___ me and it's not so bad,

   Cmaj7
It's not so bad.

Chorus 1

     G G/B   Cmaj7
And I ____want to thank you

    C/D   G   G7   Cmaj7
For giving me the best day of ___ my life.

C/D G G/B   Cmaj7
  And oh, ___ just to be with you

          Bm7   Am7
Is having the best day of my life.

Interlude

|G   G/B |Cmaj7   C/D |G   G/B |Cmaj7   C/D |

|G   G/B |Cmaj7   C/D |Bm7 |Am7 |

Bridge

           G   G/B   Cmaj7
           Push the door, I'm home ____ at last,

                  C/D   G
And I'm soaking through and through.

                      G/B   Cmaj7
And then you handed me ____ a towel,

               C/D   G
And all I see ____ is you.

                    G/B   Cmaj7
And even if my house ____ falls down ____ now,

              C/D   Bm7   Am7
I wouldn't have ____ a clue,   because you're near me.

Outro-Chorus

         G   G/B   Cmaj7
‖: And I ____want to thank you

      C/D   G   G7   Cmaj7
For giving me the best day of ____ my life.

  C/D   G   G/B   Cmaj7
   And oh, ____ just to be with you

   C/D   Bm7   Am7
Is having the best day of my life.   :‖

Toes

Words and Music by Shawn Mullins,
Zac Brown, Wyatt Durrette and
John Driskell Hopkins

Melody:

I got my toes in the wa - ter, ___ ass ___

Tune down 1/2 step:
(low to high) Eb-Ab-Db-Gb-Bb-Eb

C   F/C   G5   Gsus4   C/B   Am   G   F

Intro
| C | F/C | C | G5 Gsus4 |
| C | F/C | C Gsus4 | C |

Refrain 1

          C   F/C
I got my toes in the water, ass ___ in the sand.

          C   C/B   Am
Not a wor - ry in the world,

          G
A cold beer in my hand.

          F   Gsus4   C
Life is good ___ today,   life is good today.

Verse 1

          C   F/C
Well, the plane ___ touched down just about ___ three o'clock

          C   G5
And the cit - y's still on my mind.

          C   F/C
Bi - kinis and palm trees danced ___ in my head,

          C   G5   C
I was still ___ in the bag - gage line.

                              F/C
Concrete and cars are their own ___ prison bars

          C   G5
Like this ___ life I'm livin' in.

          C   F/C
But the plane brought me farther, I'm sur - rounded by water

          C   G5   C
And I'm ___ not go - in' back again.

<table>
<tr><td>Refrain 2</td><td>

        C   **F**
I got my toes in the water, ass ___ in the sand.

</td></tr>
</table>

Refrain 2

           C   **F**
I got my toes in the water, ass ___ in the sand.

            C   **C/B**   **Am**
Not a wor - ry in the world,

      G
A cold beer in my hand.

              F   **G5**   **C**
Life is good ___ today,   life is good today.

Chorus 1

N.C.   **F**   **C**
Adios 'n' vaya con Dios, yeah, I'm leavin' GA.

              G
And if it weren't ___ for tequila and pretty senoritas,

                    C
Ah, I'd have no reason to stay.

N.C.   **F**   **C**
  Adios 'n' vaya con Dios, yeah, I'm leavin' GA.

    G
Gonna lay in the hot sun and roll a big fat one

          N.C.
And, and grab my guitar and play.

Instrumental

|C |F/C |C |G5   Gsus4 |
|C |F/C |C Gsus4 |C |

Verse 2

                    C   **F/C**
The four days ___ flew by like a drunk ___ Friday night

               C   **G5**
As the sum - mer drew to an end.

           C   **F/C**
They ___ can't believe that I just ___ couldn't leave

               C   **G5**   **C**
And I bid ___ adieu ___ to my friends.

                         F
'Cause my bartender, she's ___ from the islands.

      C   **G5**
Her body's been kissed by the sun.

      C   **F/C**
And coconut replaces the smell ___ of the bar

               C   **G5**   **C**
And I don't ___ know if it's her ___ or the rum.

Refrain 3   *Repeat Refrain 2*

Chorus 2

N.C.   F   C
Adios 'n' vaya con Dios, a long way from GA.

        G
Yes, and all the muchachas, they call me "Big Papa"

               C
When I throw pesos their way.

N.C.   F   C
   Adios 'n' vaya con Dios, a long way from GA.

         G
Someone do me a favor and pour me some Jager

        N.C.
And,   I'll grab my guitar and play.

Interlude

| C | F/C | C | G5 Gsus4 |
| C | F/C | C Gsus4 | C | |

Chorus 3

N.C.   F   C
Adios 'n' vaya con Dios, goin' home, now, to stay.

         G
The senor - itas don't care-o when there's no dinero, yeah.

         C
I got no money to stay.

N.C.   F   C
   Adios 'n' vaya con Dios, goin' home, now, to stay.

G5
  Just gonna drive up by the lake…

Outro-Refrain

         C   F/C
And put my ass in a lawnchair, toes ___ in the clay.

        C   C/B   Am
Not a wor - ry in the world,

        G
A P.B.R. on the way.

        F/C   Gsus4   C F G C
Life is good ___ today,   life is good today.

Tom's Diner

Music and Lyrics by
Suzanne Vega

Da, da,   da, da, da, da, da, ___ da, da, da,

F#m9   F#m7   F#m   C#m   F#m*

Chorus 1

N.C.
Da, da, da, da, da, da, da, da,

Da, da, da, da, da, da, da, da.

F#m9
‖: Da, da, da, da, da, da, da, da,

F#m7   **F#m**
Da, da, da, da, da, da, da, da.   :‖ *Play 6 times*

Verse 1

N.C.(F#m)
I am sitting in the morning at the diner on the corner,

I am waiting at the counter for the man to pour the coffee,

And he fills it only half way and before I even argue

He is looking out the window at somebody coming in.

Chorus 2   ‖: Da, da, da, da, da, da, da, da,

F♯m9

F♯m7   F♯m
Da, da, da, da, da, da, da, da.   :‖

Verse 2

N.C.(F♯m)
"It is always nice to see you," says the man behind the counter,

To the woman who has come in. She is shaking her umbrella.

C♯m F♯m*   N.C.(F♯m)
And I look the other way as they are kissing their hellos.

  C♯m   F♯m*   N.C.(F♯m)
And I'm pre - tending not to see them, and in - stead I pour the milk.

Chorus 3   *Repeat Chorus 2*

Verse 3

N.C.(F♯m)
I open up the paper. There's a story of an actor

Who has died while he was drinking, it was no one I had heard of.

C♯m F♯m*   C♯m   F♯m*
And I'm turning to the horoscope ___ and looking for the funnies,

C♯m F♯m*   C♯m   F♯m*
But I'm feeling someone watching me and so I raise my head.

Chorus 4

          F#m9
‖: Da, da, da, da, da, da, da, da,

    F#m7   F#m
Da, da, da, da, da, da, da, da. :‖ *Play 4 times*

Verse 4

C#m F#m*   N.C.(F#m)
      There's a woman on the outside looking inside.

Does she see me? No, she does not really see me,

'Cause she sees her own reflection.
C#m   F#m*   N.C.(F#m)
  And I'm trying not to notice that she's inching up her skirt.
C#m   F#m*
And while she's straightening her stockings, her hair has gotten wet.

Chorus 5   *Repeat Chorus 2*

Verse 5

N.C.(F#m)
      Oh, this rain, it will continue through the morning

As I'm list'ning to the bells of the cathedral.
F#m9 N.C.(F#m)
  I am thinking of your voice.

Outro-Chorus   *Repeat Chorus 2 and fade*

Trouble

Words and Music by
Ray LaMontagne

Melody:

Trou-ble, _____   trou-ble, trou - ble,

G   C/G   D/A   Dsus4/A   C   Dsus2/A   F   Am7

D7   D7sus4   D7sus2/A   D7sus2   G/B   Bm   Am

Intro
```
:‖: G   C/G │ G   D/A   Dsus4/A   D/A   :‖   Play 4 times
```

Verse 1

```
G        D/A  G              C/G
```
Trouble, ____ trouble, trouble, ____ trouble, trouble.

```
G           D/A
```
Trouble been doggin' my soul

```
            C                    G  D/A  Dsus2/A  D/A
```
Since the day I was born, ah.

```
G        D/A  G        C/G
```
Worry, ____ worry, worry, worry, worry.

```
G           D/A                        C
```
Worry just will not seem to leave my mind alone.

Chorus 1

```
G  D/A   N.C.        G              C
```
Well, I've been, uh, saved by ____ a woman.

```
F  C         G              C
```
I've been, uh, saved by ____ a woman.

```
F  C         G              C
```
I've been, uh, saved by ____ a woman.

```
F  C         Am7               D7
```
She won't let me go, she won't let me go, now.

```
D7sus4  D7  D7sus2/A   Am7
```
She won't let me go

```
        D7                D7sus2
```
She won't let me go now, now.

Interlude 1   ‖: G   C/G │G   D/A   Dsus4/A   D/A   :‖

Verse 2
G   D/A   G   C/G
Trouble, ___ oh, ___ trouble, trou - ble, trouble, trouble.

G   D/A
Feels like ev'ry time I get back on my feet,

                      C   G   D/A   Dsus2/A   D/A
She come around ___ and knock me down a - gain.

G   D/A   G   C/G
Worry, ___ oh, ___ wor - ry, worry, worry, worry.

G   D/A   C
Sometimes I swear it feels like this worry ___ is my only friend.

Chorus 2
G D/A   N.C.   G   C
Well, I've been, uh, saved by ___ a woman.

F C   G   C
I've been, uh, saved by ___ a woman.

F C   G   C
I've been, uh, saved by ___ a woman.

G/B   Am7   D7
She won't let me go, she won't let me go, now.

D7sus4 D7 D7sus2/A   Am7
She won't let me go,

        D7
She won't let me go now, now.

Bridge

        C   Bm Am G
        Oh, ____   ah,

        C   Bm
        Oh.

        Am   G   C/G G
        Mm, she good ____ to me, now.

        C/G   G   C/G   G
        She give me love ____ and af - fection.

        C/G   G   C/G G
        Say she good ____ to me, now.

        C/G   G   C/G   G
        She give me love ____ and af - fection.

        C/G   G   C/G   G
        I said, I love her.   Yes, I love her.

        C/G   G   C/G   G C/G
        I said, I love her.   I said, I love.

           G   C/G G
        She good ____ to me, now.

        C/G G   C/G   G   C/G
        She good to me.   She good to me.

Outro

        G   C/G G C/G G
        Mm, _____ mm,

        C/G G C/G G C/G G
        Mm, ____ mm.

Torn

Words and Music by Phil Thornalley,
Scott Cutler and Anne Previn

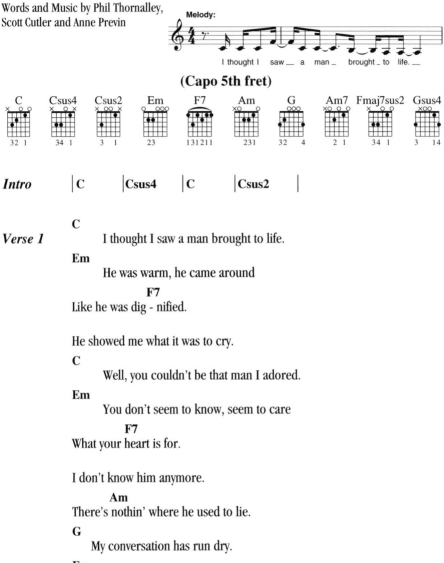

Melody:

I thought I saw __ a man __ brought __ to life. __

(Capo 5th fret)

C   Csus4   Csus2   Em   F7   Am   G   Am7   Fmaj7sus2   Gsus4

Intro | C | Csus4 | C | Csus2 |

Verse 1

       C
I thought I saw a man brought to life.

  Em
He was warm, he came around

      F7
Like he was dig - nified.

He showed me what it was to cry.

C
Well, you couldn't be that man I adored.

  Em
You don't seem to know, seem to care

      F7
What your heart is for.

I don't know him anymore.

    Am
There's nothin' where he used to lie.

G
My conversation has run dry.

  Em
That's what's going on.

G   C
Nothing's fine, I'm torn.

Chorus 1

    C   G
I'm all out of faith,

             Am7
This is how I feel.

                    Fmaj7sus2
I'm cold and I am shamed

               C
Lying naked on the floor.

               G   Am7
Illusion never changed__ into something real.

I'm wide awake

    Fmaj7sus2   C
And I__ can see the perfect sky is torn.

            G
You're a little late,

           Am7   Fmaj7sus2
I'm already torn.

Verse 2

 C
So, I guess the fortune teller's right.

Em
   I should've seen just what was there

       F7
And not some holy light.

But you crawled beneath my veins, and now

Am
I don't care, I have no luck.

G
   I don't miss it all that much.

Em   G
   There's just so many things

             C
That I can't touch. I'm torn.

<pre>
                C   G
Chorus 2   I'm all out of faith,

                         Am7
              This is how I feel.

                              Fmaj7sus2
              I'm cold and I am shamed

                              C
              Lying naked on the floor.

                              G   Am7
              Illusion never changed__ into something real.

              I'm wide awake

                  Fmaj7sus2   C
              And I__ can see the perfect sky is torn.

                              G
              You're a little late,

                          Am7   Fmaj7sus2
              I'm already torn.

              Am7   Fmaj7sus2
              Torn.

                  Am   C   G
Interlude   Oo, oo.
</pre>

	Am
Verse 3	There's nothing where he used to lie.

        G
            My inspiration has run dry.

      Em
             That's what's going on.

      G
             Nothing's right, I'm torn.

Chorus 3   **Repeat Chorus 1**

            G
Outro   I'm all out of faith,

            Am7
     This is how I feel.

                  Fmaj7sus2
     I'm cold and I'm ashamed,

                  C
     Bound and broken on the floor.

            G
     You're a little late.

            Am7   **Fmaj7sus2**
     I'm already torn.

     Am7   **G**   **Gsus4**
     Torn.   Oh.

     |**C** |**G** |**Am7** |**Fmaj7sus2** |

The Way I Am

Words and Music by
Ingrid Michaelson

Melody:

If you __ were fall - ing, __

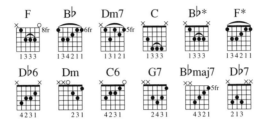

F   Bb   Dm7   C   Bb*   F*

Db6   Dm   C6   G7   Bbmaj7   Db7

Intro

‖: N.C.(F) |(Bb) |(Dm7) |(C)   :‖

Verse 1

N.C.(F)   (Bb)   (Dm7)   (C)
If you were fal - ling,   then I would catch you.

(F)   (Bb)   (Dm7)   (C)
You need a light, ___   I'd find a match.

Chorus 1

N.C.(Bb)   (C)   (F)   (Dm7)
'Cause I   love the way ___ you say good morn - ing,

(Bb)   (Db6)   (C)   (F)
And you   take me the way I am.

Verse 2

```
        F                Bb Dm7           C
     If you are chill - y,    here, take my sweater.
        F                 Bb  Dm7          C
        Your head is ach - ing,   I'll make it better.
```

Chorus 2

```
           Bb* C             F*               Dm7
     'Cause I      love the way ___ you call me "ba - by,"
           Bb* Db6             F*
        And you  take me the way I am.
```

Verse 3

```
        F                Bb    Dm7           C              F
        I'd buy you Ro - gaine    when you start losing all your hair.
                   Bb Dm7         C
        Sew on patch - es    to all you tear.
```

Chorus 3

```
           Bb* C                    F*              Dm7
     'Cause I      love you more than I ___ could ever prom - ise,
           Bb* Db6            Dm C6
        And you  take me the way I am.  Mm.
        Bb* Db6               Dm      G7
        You  take me the way I ___ am. Mm.
        Bbmaj7 Db7         C    F*
        You      take me the way I am.
```

What I Am

Words and Music by Brandon Aly,
Edie Brickell, John Bush, John Houser
and Kenneth Withrow

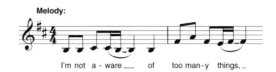

Melody:

I'm not a - ware ___ of too man - y things, _

Bsus2   Dsus2   Asus2   Em   D

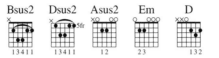

Intro   ‖: Bsus2   Dsus2 │   │Asus2   │Bsus2   :‖

Verse 1
         Bsus2   **Dsus2**
I'm not aware of ____ too many things,

        Asus2   **Bsus2**   **Dsus2 Asus2 Bsus2**
I know what I know, if you know what I mean.

Verse 2   *Repeat Verse 1*

Verse 3
          Bsus2   **Dsus2 Asus2**   **Bsus2**
Philos - ophy   is the talk on a cereal box.

            Dsus2 Asus2   **Bsus2**
Religion   is the smile on a dog.

Verse 4
        Bsus2   **Dsus2**
I'm not aware of ____ too many things,

        Asus2   **Bsus2**
I know what I know, if you know what I mean.

        Dsus2   **Asus2 Bsus2**
  Do ya?

Pre-Chorus 1
        Em   **D**
Choke me in the shallow water,

        Em   **D**
Be - fore I get too deep.

Chorus 1

Bsus2   Dsus2
What I am is what I am,

Asus2   Bsus2
Are you what you are or what?

Dsus2
What I am is what I am,

Asus2   Bsus2
Are you what you are? Oh.

Verse 5   *Repeat Verse 1*

Verse 6

Bsus2   Dsus2 Asus2   Bsus2
Philos - ophy   is a walk on the slippery rocks.

Dsus2 Asus2   Bsus2
Religion   is a light in the fog.

Verse 7   *Repeat Verse 4*

Pre-Chorus 2

Em   D
‖: Choke me in the shallow water,

Em   D
Be - fore I get too deep. :‖

Chorus 2

Bsus2   Dsus2
‖: What I am is what I am,

Asus2   Bsus2
Are you what you are or what?   :‖

Dsus2
What I am is what I am,

Asus2   Bsus2
Are you what you are or what ___ you are is

Dsus2
What I am is what I am,

Asus2   Bsus2
Are you what you or ___ what?

Pre-Chorus 3

Em		D	

Ha, la, da,　　da.　　　　　　　　　　　　　　I

Em		D	

Say, I say, I say,　　　　　I　do. Hey, hey, hey, hey, hey, hey.

Guitar Solo　　‖: Bsus2　Dsus2 |　　| Asus2　| Bsus2　:‖ *Play 8 times*

Pre-Chorus 4　　*Repeat Pre-Chorus 2*

Pre-Chorus 5

　　　　Bsus2　　　　Dsus2
‖: Choke me in the shallow water,

　　　Asus2　　　　Bsus2
Be - fore I get too deep.　　　:‖

　　　　　　　　Dsus2
Choke me in the shallow water,

　　　Asus2　　　Bsus2 Dsus2 Asus2
Be - fore I get too ___　　deep.

　　　Bsus2
‖:　Don't let me get too deep.

Dsus2　　　　　Asus2　　Bsus2
　Don't let me get too deep.　:‖

Outro　　*Repeat Chorus 1 w/ vocal ad lib. till fade*

What I Got

Words and Music by Brad Nowell,
Eric Wilson, Floyd Gaugh and
Lindon Roberts

Melody:

Ear - ly   in   the morn - in',

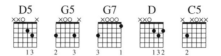

Intro | D5   G5 | D5   G5 |

Verse 1
D5   G5   D5   G5
Early in the morn - in', risin' to the street.

D5   G5
Light me up that cigarette and I

D5   G5
Strap shoes on my feet. (De, de, de, de, de.)

D5   G5   D5   G5
Got to find a rea - son, reason things went wrong.

D5   G5   D5   G5
Got to find a reason why my money's all gone.

D5   G5   D5   G5
I ____ got a Dalma - tion and I can still get high.

D5   G5   D5   G5
I ____ can play the guitar like a motherfuckin' riot.

Interlude 1   ‖: D5   G5 | D5   G5 :‖

Verse 2

      D5   **G5**
Well, life is (too short) so love ____ the one you got

        D5   **G5**
'Cause you might get run over or you might get shot.

D5   **G5**
Never start no static, I just get it off my (chest.)

D5   **G5**
Never had to battle with no bulletproof (vest.)

D5   **G5**
Take a small example, take a ti-ti-ti-tip from me.

D5   **G5**
Take all of your money, give it all (to char-i-ty-ty-ty-ty.)

      D5   **G5**
Love is what I got, it's within my reach

        D5   **G5**
And the Sublime style's still straight ____ from Long Beach.

          D5   **G5**
It all comes ____ back to you, you fin'lly get what you deserve.

D5   **G5**
Try to test that, you're bound to get served.

D5   **G5**
Loves what I got, don't start a riot.

      D5   **G5**
You feel it when the dance gets hot.

Chorus 1

D5 **G5**   **D5**   **G5**
Lovin'   is what I got. ____ I said re - member that.

D5 **G5**   **D5**   **G5**
Lovin'   is what I got, ____ and re - member that.

D5 **G5**   **D5**   **G7**
Lovin'   is what I got. ____ I said re - member that.

D   **G5**   **D**   **G7**
Lovin'   is what I got, ____ I got, I got, ____ I got.

	D5 **G5**
Verse 3	Why, I don't cry when my dog runs away.

D5   **G5**
I don't get angry at the bills I have to pay.

D5   **G5**
I don't get angry when my mom smokes pot,

D5   **G5**
Hits the bottle and moves right to the rock.

D5   **G5**
Fuckin' and fightin', it's all the same.

      D5   **G5**
Livin' with Louie Dog's the only way to stay sane.

D5   **G5**   **D5**
    Let the lovin', let the lovin' come back ____ to me.

Interlude 2   ‖: **D5**   **C5** **G5** | **D5**   **C5** **G5** :‖ **D5** | |

              D5 **C5** **G5**   **D5**   **C5**   **G5**
Chorus 2   'Cause lovin'   is what I got. ____ I said re - member that.

            D5 **C5** **G5**   **D5**   **C5**   **G5**
Lov - in'   is what I got, ____ and re - member that.

            D5 **C5** **G5**   **D5**   **C5**   **G5**
Lov - in'   is what I got. ____ I said re - member that.

            D5 **C5** **G5**   **D5**   **C5**   **G5**
Lov - in'   is what I got, ____ I got, I got, ____ I got.

Outro | **D5**   **G5** | **D5**   **G7** | **D**   ‖

Who Will Save Your Soul

Lyrics and Music by
Jewel Kilcher

Melody:

Peo-ple liv-ing their lives for you __ on T. - V., __

Am   C   G   D   Asus2   Cadd9   Dsus4   Gsus4

Intro
| N.C.(Am) | (C) | (G) | (D) |

Verse 1

  Asus2   **Am** **Cadd9**
People living their lives for you on TV,

C   **G**   **Dsus4** **D**
They say they're better than you and you agree.

Asus2   **Am**   **Cadd9**   **C**
He says, "Hold my calls," from behind those cold brick walls.

  G   **Dsus4** **D**
Says, "Come here, boy, there ain't nothing for free."

Asus2   **Am**   **Cadd9**   **C**   **G**
Another doc - tor's bill, a lawyer's bill, another cute, cheap thrill.

             Dsus4
You know you love him if you put him in your will.

Chorus 1

D Asus2 Am Cadd9 C   **G**
But who will save   your souls

     Dsus4   **D**
When it comes ____ to the flowers, now?

Asus2 Am **Cadd9**   **C**   **G**
Who, ____ who ____ will save your souls

     Dsus4   **D**
After those lies ____ that you told, boy?

Asus2 **Am Cadd9 C**   **G**
And who will save _____ your ___ souls

     Dsus4   **D**
If you won't ____ save your own?

Asus2   **Am**
La, da, da, da, di, da, da,

Cadd9 **C** **G Dsus4 D**
Da, da, da, ya, di.

Verse 2

Asus2   Am   Cadd9   C
We try to hustle ____ them, try to bust - le them, try to cuss them.

G   Dsus4   D
The cops want *someone to bust down on* Or - leans Avenue.

Asus2   Am   Cadd9
Another day, another dollar, another war,

C   Gsus4   G   Dsus4   D
Another tower went up where the home - less had their homes.

Asus2   Am   Cadd9   C   G
So we pray to as many diff'rent gods as there are flowers,

Dsus4   D
But we call re - ligion our friend.

Asus2   Am   Cadd9
We're so worried about a saving our souls,

C   G   Dsus4
Afraid that God will take His toll, that we for - get to begin.

Chorus 2

D Asus2 Am Cadd9 C   G
But   who will save   your souls

Dsus4   D
When it comes ____ to the betters, now?

Asus2 Am   Cadd9   C   G
Who, ____ who ____ will save your souls

Dsus4   D
After those lies ____ that you told, boy?

Asus2   Am Cadd9 C   G
And who will   save   your souls

Dsus4   D
If you won't ____ save your own?

Am
La, da, da, da, di, da, da,

Cadd9   C   G Dsus4 D
Da, da, da, ya, di.

Interlude ‖: N.C.(Em) | :‖

Verse 3
Asus2   Am   Cadd9   C
Some are walk - ing, some are talk - ing, some are stalk - ing their kill.

G   Dsus4
Got Social Security, but it doesn't pay your bills.

D   Asus2   Am   Cadd9
There are ad - dictions to feed and there are   mouths to pay,

C   Gsus4   G   Dsus4
So you bar - gain with the devil, but you're O - K for today.

D Asus2   Am   Cadd9
Say   that you love them, take their money and run.

C   G   Dsus4   D   Asus2
Say "It's been swell, sweetheart, but it was   just one of those things,

            Am   Cadd9
Those flings, those strings you   got to cut,

C   G   Dsus4   D   Asus2
So get out   on the streets, girls, and bust your ____ butts."

Chorus 3
        Am Cadd9 C G
Who will save _____

        Dsus4 D Asus2 Am Cadd9 C   G
Your _____ soul?

            Dsus4   D
Baby, come, ____ little ba - by, yeah.

Outro ‖: Asus2 Am │Cadd9   C |
│ G   │Dsus4   D   :‖ *Repeat and fade*
                                    w/ lead vocal ad lib.

Wonderwall

Words and Music by
Noel Gallagher

Melody:

To - day   is gon - na be the day that they're

(Capo 2nd fret)

Em7   G   Dsus4   A7sus4   Cadd9   C   D   D/F#   Em11

Intro

‖: Em7   G | Dsus4   A7sus4 :‖   *Play 4 times*

Verse 1

Em7   G
Today is gon-na be the day

      Dsus4   A7sus4
That they're gonna throw it back to you.

Em7   G
  By now you should have somehow

  Dsus4   A7sus4
Real-ized what you gotta do.

Em7   G
I don't believe that an - ybody

Dsus4   A7sus4   Cadd9 Dsus4 A7sus4
Feels the way I do about you now.

Verse 2

Em7   G
  Backbeat, the word is on the street

  Dsus4   A7sus4
That the fire in your heart is out.

Em7   G
  I'm sure you've heard it all before,

  Dsus4   A7sus4
But you never really had a doubt.

Em7   G
I don't believe that an-ybody

Dsus4   A7sus4   Em7 G Dsus4 A7sus4
Feels the way I do about you now.

	C	D	Em7
Chorus 1	And all ___ the roads we have ___ to walk are wind - ing,		

| | C | D | Em7 |

And all ___ the lights that lead ___ us there are blind - ing.

C   **D**

There are many things ___ that I would

G   **D/F♯**   **Em7**   **G**   **A7sus4**

Like to say to you, ___ but I don't know how.

        Cadd9 Em7 G   **Em7**

Because maybe _____ you're gon-na

          Cadd9   **Em7**   **G**

Be the one that saves me.

       Em7   **Cadd9 Em7 G**   **Em7**   **Cadd9 Em7**

And af - ter all _____ you're my wonderwall.

| **G**   **Em7** | | **Em11** |

	Em7	G	
Verse 3	Today was gon-na be the day,		

       Dsus4   **A7sus4**

But they'll never throw it back to you.

Em7   **G**

By now you should have somehow

    Dsus4   **A7sus4**

Real-ized what you're not to do.

Em7   **G**

I don't believe that an-ybody

Dsus4   **A7sus4**   **Em7 G Dsus4 A7sus4**

Feels the way I do about you now.

Chorus 2

```
          C                    D              Em7
And all ___ the roads that lead ___ you there were wind - ing,
          C                    D              Em7
And all ___ the lights that light ___ the way are blind - ing.
C                    D
There are many things ___ that I would
G      D/F♯    Em7      G            A7sus4
Like to say to you, ___ but I don't know how.
         Cadd9 Em7 G           Em7
I said maybe _____ you're gon-na
              Cadd9  Em7  G
Be the one that saves me.
         Em7 Cadd9 Em7 G
And af - ter all
             Em7        Cadd9 Em7  G  Em7
You're my wonderwall.
         Cadd9 Em7 G           Em7
I said maybe _____ you're gon-na
              Cadd9   Em7  G
Be the one that saves me.
         Em7 Cadd9 Em7 G
And af - ter all
             Em7        Cadd9 Em7  G  Em7
You're my won - derwall.
         Cadd9 Em7 G           Em7
I said maybe _____ you're gon-na
              Cadd9   Em7  G
Be the one that saves me.
             Em7            Cadd9 Em7 G
You're gon-na be the one that saves me.
             Em7            Cadd9 Em7  G  Em7
You're gon-na be the one that saves me.
```

Outro

```
‖: Cadd9    Em7  | G      Em7   :‖  Play 3 times
 | Cadd9    Em7  | G      Em7   |
```

Yellow

Words and Music by Guy Berryman,
Jon Buckland, Will Champion
and Chris Martin

Melody:

Look at the stars,

Tuning:
(low to high) E–A–B–G–B–D♯

B   Badd11   F♯6   Emaj7   G♯m   Eadd9   B*   F♯m11

Intro

B		Badd11	B		Badd11
B		Badd11	F♯6		
Emaj7			B		Badd11

Verse 1

    B   F♯6
Look at the stars, look how they shine for ____ you,

                    Emaj7
And ev'rything you do, ____ yeah, they were all yellow.

    B   F♯6
I came along, I wrote a song for ____ you,

                    Emaj7   B
And all the things you do, ____ and it was called yellow.

Badd11   **F♯6**
So then I took my ____ turn,

                    Emaj7
Oh, what a thing to've done,

                    B Badd11 B
And it was all yellow.

Emaj7   **G♯m**   **F♯6**   **Emaj7**
Your skin, ____ oh yeah, your skin and bones,

    G♯m   **F♯6**
Turn in - to some-thing beautiful.

Emaj7   **G♯m**   **F♯6**   **Emaj7**
And you know, ____ you know I love you so,

Eadd9
You know I love you so.

Interlude 1　|B　　|　　|F#6　|　　|
　　　　　　　|Emaj7　|　　|B　　|　　|

Verse 2

B　　　　　　　　　　　　　　　F#6
　　I swam across, I jumped across for ___ you,
　　　　　　　　　　　　Emaj7
Oh, what a thing to do, ___ 'cause you were all yellow.
　　B　　　　　　Badd11　　　F#6
　　I drew a line, I drew a line for ___ you,
　　　　　　　　　　　　Emaj7　　　　　　　B　Badd11　B
Oh, what a thing to do, ___ and it was all yellow.
Emaj7　　　G#m　　　　F#6　　　　　Emaj7
　　Your skin, ___ oh yeah, your skin and bones,
　　　G#m　　　　F#6
Turn in - to some-thing beautiful.
Emaj7　　　　G#m　　　　F#6　　　　　Emaj7
　　And you know, ___ for you I'd bleed myself dry,
Eadd9　　　　　　　　　　B
　　For you I'd bleed myself dry.

Interlude 2　　Repeat Interlude 1

Chorus

　　　B　　　　　　　　　　　　F#6
It's true, look how they shine for you,
　　　　　　　　　　　　Emaj7
Look how they shine for you,
　　　　　　　　　　　　B
Look how they shine for,
　　　　　　　　　　　F#6
Look how they shine for you,
　　　　　　　　　　　Emaj7
Look how they shine for you,

Look how they shine.

Outro

　　B*
　　　Look at the stars,
　　　　　　　　F#m11
Look how they shine for ___ you,
　　　　　　　　Emaj7
And all the things that you ___ do.

You Learn

Lyrics by Alanis Morissette
Music by Alanis Morissette
and Glen Ballard

Melody:

I _____ rec-om-mend get-tin' your heart

(Capo 1st fret)

Gsus4   G   Fsus4   F   Cadd9   Dadd$^4_9$ G5   Dsus4   Dsus4*

	Gsus4 G Fsus4 F	
Intro	Oo, ____ oo, ____ ow.	
	Gsus4 G Fsus4 F	
	Oo.	

	Gsus4 G Fsus4 F
Verse 1	I ___ recom - mend gettin' your heart trampled on
	Gsus4 G Fsus4 F
	To anyone, yeah, ____ oh.
	Gsus4 G Fsus4 F
	I ___ recom - mend walkin' a - round
	Gsus4 G Fsus4 F
	Naked in your livin' room, ____ yeah.

	Cadd9 Dadd$^4_9$
Pre-Chorus 1	Swallow it down. ___ (What a jagged little pill.)
	Cadd9 Dadd$^4_9$
	It feels so good ___ (Swimmin' in your stomach.)
	Cadd9 Dadd$^4_9$
	Wait until the dust settles.

Chorus 1

G5   Dsus4
You live, you learn. You love, you learn.

                 G5
You cry, you learn.   You lose, you learn.

                                  Dsus4 G5
You bleed, you learn. You scream, you learn.

Verse 2

         Gsus4 G   Fsus4
Oh, oh. ___ I ___ recom - mend

           F   Gsus4 G
Biting off more than you can chew to anyone.

Fsus4   F
I ___ certainly do, ___ oh.

Gsus4 G   Fsus4
  I ___ recom - mend

               F   Gsus4 G
Stickin' your foot in your mouth at any time.

Fsus4 F
  Feel free.

Pre-Chorus 2

Cadd9   Dadd$^4_9$
  Throw it down. ___ (The caution blocks you from the wind.)

Cadd9   Dadd$^4_9$
Hold it up ___ (To the rays.)

Cadd9   Dadd$^4_9$
You wait and see ___ when the smoke clears.

Chorus 2

G5   Dsus4
You live, you learn. You love, you learn.

       G5
You cry, you learn. You lose, you learn.

             Dsus4 G5
You bleed, you learn. You scream, you learn. ____ Oh, oh.

Interlude   ‖: G5 | :‖ *Play 4 times w/ vocal ad lib.*

Pre-Chorus 3

Cadd9 Dadd$^4_9$
Wear it out, ____(The way a three-year-old would do.)

Cadd9 Dadd$^4_9$ Cadd9
Melt it down, ____(You're gonna have to eventually any - way.)

      Dadd$^4_9$
The fire trucks ____ are comin' up around the bend.

Chorus 3   *Repeat Chorus 1*

Outro

G   Gsus4 G   Dsus4*
You grieve, you learn. You choke, ____ you learn.

        G5   G
You laugh, you learn. You choose, you learn.

          Dsus4*
You pray, you learn. You ask, you learn.

       G5
You live, you learn. Ah.